Hi

Eliot

ELIOT'S ARK

ELIOT'S ARK

by *Sonny Eliot*

Illustrations by Charles Herzog III

Wayne State University Press • *Detroit* • *1972*

Published simultaneously in Canada
by the Copp Clark Publishing Company
517 Wellington Street, West
Toronto 2B, Canada.

Grateful acknowledgment is extended to the Detroit News for permission to reprint these articles.

Library of Congress Cataloging in Publication Data
Eliot, Sonny, 1922–
Eliot's Ark, by Sonny Eliot
Illus. by Charles Herzog III
A collection of articles from the author's weekly column in the
Detroit News.
1. animals 2. animals-anecdotes, facetiae, satire, etc.
I. Herzog, Charles, 1920–illus. II. Detroit News III. title.
QL50.E45 1972   590'.744'34   72-6777
ISBN-0-8143-1487-2

CONTENTS

FOREWORD

This book is written by Marvin Eliot—known as "Sonny" Eliot, as you may have read on the cover. He is a noted radio and television personality in the Detroit area. *Eliot's Ark* was conceived, grew in-utero, and was born as a result of his ten years experience as mastermind of "At the Zoo," a weekly TV visit to the Detroit Zoological Park.

Sonny has had a long and varied career. His TV weather show has a prodigious following, consisting of everyone from chairbound oldsters to hip teenagers. His forecasts are larded with clever jokes, temperatures in mispronounced foreign languages, and horribly butchered names of small Michigan towns. I am amazed that he has produced such a fine book because he usually spells *fog* "PHAWG."

The book will appeal to all segments of the reading public, ranging from the "tearful" animal lover to the guy who whacks pigeons with his umbrella and kicks cats. Sonny has spent a lot of time putting his "Ark" together. It represents countless hours of research and an able application of practical knowledge.

Rarely can I appear on his zoo program because I usually find myself elbowed out of camera range; and if I stand my ground he stands behind me, makes faces, sticks out his tongue, and waggles his ears. Still, Sonny is a great guy and I love him. I have even read and enjoyed *Eliot's Ark.*

Robert F. Willson, D.V.M., Director
Detroit Zoological Park
Royal Oak, Michigan

THERE'S NO BITE IN THIS FELLOW

Armadillo

Way back when a Spanish adventurer named Cortez and his pantalooned plunderers came to the New World to see what they could see, they not only copped a peek at the Pacific, assayed the Aztecs, and glommed onto the gold, they also took note of the many strange and wonderful animals living in the neighborhood. One of the strangest was a quaint, queer, quick creature that looked like a lady's purse with legs. It impressed the Spaniards because it seemed to be wearing a coat of armor, much the same as they did, and so they called this animal the *armadillo* or "little armored thing."

You'd think that with all this armor, the armadillo would be one heck of a fighter, able to slash, bite, scratch and still remain safe within his shield. Forget it, he's not a fighter at all. Lover, yes, fighter, no. He can't even bite, because his teeth are way back in his mouth, none in the front. However, it doesn't seem to hamper his eating too much. Mostly he dines on white ants, or termites, and then varies the menu with a crunchy scorpion, a tasty snake, a furry mouse, a smooth egg, or maybe a salad of some sort of vegetable matter. The diet may not be balanced too well, but you'll have to give him credit for variety. And who ever heard of an armadillo asking for a Tums?

If old Armorplate is threatened, he usually runs in a short-legged scurry trying to make the safety of his burrow. Occasionally, if he can spare the time, and the ground is soft, he'll quickly bury himself, and if this doesn't work, he'll curl up into a ball and hope his thick hide discourages the wild dog or fox. Of course, the wild dog or fox is no dummy, he knows that he can roll the armadillo over and get at his not-so-protected abdomen, or sometimes push him into a pool of water where he unrolls to breathe and finds that he doesn't have too much longer to breathe anyhow.

There are many kinds of armadillos living today, varying somewhat in size and shape, but looking pretty much the same nonetheless. They all have the same method for looking like a miniature tank with a live head. The shell encases the back, not a part of the skeleton, like a lobster's, but actually hardened skin in the form of horny plates and covered with bony scales. Bands across the middle sort of act like hinges so that they can bend, turn, and twist without their underwear creeping up. They have a turret-topped head too, and some even have their tails sheathed. The only thing they don't do is clank.

NO MATTER WHAT—HE'S STILL A BOAR

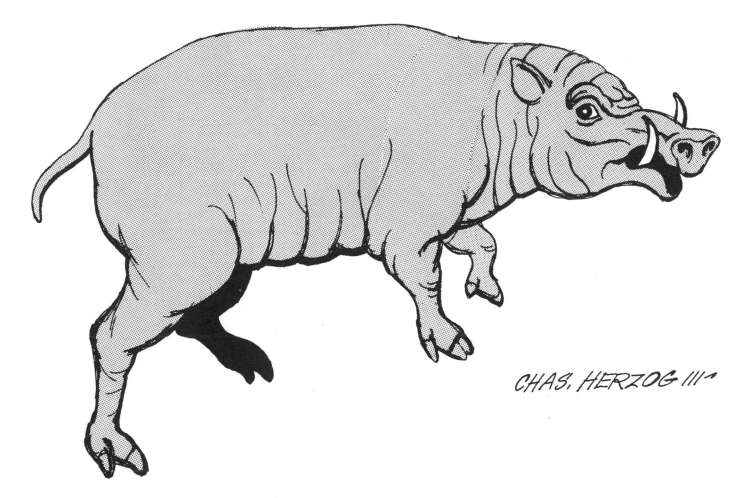

CHAS. HERZOG III

Babiroussa

A chrysanthemum by any other name would be easier to spell, and a babiroussa by any other name would be called a wild boar, one of the most interesting and confounding members of the hog family. There are several kinds of wild swine, such as the Indian, or crested wild boar, and the Eurasian wild boar, none of which would fill you with a sense of beauty, unless you're related to someone with a tough gristle-like snout and curling tusks.

Ordinarily when you refer to pigs you call the male a *boar* and the female a *sow*, but it's different when dealing with the wild species—then they're all boars, both male and female. Anyhow, the babiroussa, pictured here, is one of the most unlovely creatures in the jungle. He's hairless, could use a body stocking made of hair, has gray, wrinkled skin, and is streamlined, but in the wrong direction. In other words he's wedge-shaped from the rear to the front, tapering down from big, broad hindquarters to low, narrow shoulders and a small head. If he ever wanted to sell his brain, he could advertise it as slightly used.

His strangely shaped tusks are a dentist's delight, but the weirdest thing of all is that they serve no purpose, have no use, and are about as much help as a shoeshine boy in a nudist camp. And poor Mr. Babiroussa has to consider them a frightful bore for a boar, because they grow straight upward, go through the upper lip, and then curl backward, sometimes even touching his forehead! Some of the tusks have been measured at a length of seventeen inches! And that's the tooth, the whole tooth, and nothing but the tooth.

This wild woodland wanderer lives near the water in the jungle because he just loves to swim, swimming better than an otter's daughter, which is pretty good for a 125 pound, two foot high pig. And there are records of this unappealing creature being domesticated. Ah, but his cousin, the Eurasian wild boar, is hardly as tractable. This boar is a 350 pound, five feet long, three feet tall animal with the disposition of an untipped cab driver. He has long, black, coarse hair that covers a thick, wooly, yellowish-brown underfur, and tusks that are sharp, strong, and could be a foot long.

The Eurasian boar is the one that's got the deserved reputation of being ferocious enough to take on a whole pack of dogs and come out the winner. He'll even charge a horse and rider, slash at the horse's legs, knock it down, and then make a believer as well as an invalid of the hunter. In the Middle Ages killing the wild boar was considered an act of chivalry that took great courage. Of course, in those days they gave the old diehard fighter a chance. They didn't have guns, just guts, and long lances!

VAMPIRES NEED TWO FRONT TEETH

Vampire Bat

Think of something that makes your skin crawl, your heart pound, your blood race, your hair stand on end, and is as dangerous as standing at the wrong end of a shooting gallery. No, not a woman driver! We're talking about a flying mammal called a vampire bat.

The vampire bat, a gruesome little horror that gave Bram Stoker the idea for his chilling Dracula, actually doesn't suck blood, but he does lap it up greedily. If they find a sleeping animal they'll land nearby and scuttle towards it like some huge, hairy spider. And you thought little Miss Muffet was a sissy!

The vampires have two front teeth, from the song of the same name, which are especially modified for their nasty little dinners. They scoop a trough in the skin and then move about so the head rests at the bottom of this wound, and when the trickle begins, so does dinner. The teeth are sharp enough so that the incision is almost painless and the victim is rarely awakened by the attack. This, of course, doesn't include insomniacs who are awakened by the "something," like the scream of a distraught butterfly.

They sleep in caves, hollow trees, old houses, and just about any other place they can find to hang their heads. They range from Argentina to the Southern United States in countless millions, and they seem to be gradually extending their range northward. Now, isn't that good news?

Actually, they are a serious threat to man and other domestic animals, because they transmit a great number of diseases along with their bite, being responsible for outbreaks of rabies in Central America. The economics of South American countries have been affected by the vampires that attach on cattle, for instance. Many South American Indians believe that this furry monster is the reason for the extinction of the original wild American horse.

He's not too discriminating in his taste. He'll even take tired blood---from human beings or domestic animals, or from any other imaginable animal as well, from toads to jaguars. The only prerequisite this squeaking nightmare has is that his victim be alive!

The vampire bat has one real claim to fame though, and even that's as popular as a fishhook in the thumb. He's the only mammal that is a true parasite. Next to him a flea seems like a nice guy.

It's also reported, although not yet completely verified, that the vampire will flutter in the face of a potential victim, emitting a soothing scent to calm the prey before sinking his incisors. Think of that, men, the next time a shapely thing glides by trailing about five bucks' worth of Arpege.

MOTHER NATURE'S TEDDY BEAR

Koala Bear

Way back in the year 1902, the year they developed cellophane shirts for businessmen who wanted to watch their waistlines, there was a newspaper cartoon of Teddy Roosevelt holding a grizzly bear cub. An enterprising toy manufacturer designed a cuddly toy bear which he called Teddy's bear, and in no time at all it was known as Teddy Bear, and a mighty popular thing for kids to go to bed with. But, like all man-made things, old Mama Nature beat the enterprising toy manufacturer to the punch by designing one of the most charming, furry, and lovable little animals on earth, the koala bear.

He's not really a bear at all, he merely happens to look like one, no relation at all. He has no tail, has large bushy ears, a relatively big, black nose, and small bright eyes and a permanently perplexed expression, as though he were looking for the horse in horse radish. He's not very large either, barely three feet long and rarely weighing more than twenty-five pounds. He's a child's delight, making a wonderful pet for as long as he lives, which isn't too long in captivity. Not really recommended as a pet.

This living toy takes a long time to grow up into adulthood. When he's born he's only about an inch long and almost as thick around as a lead pencil, and never more than one to the litter, which makes for a mighty small litter. Mama Koala then puts her tiny baby into her pouch, because Mama Koala is a marsupial who lives only in Australia, and lets the baby take his own sweet time growing up.

By the age of six months, he's finally got a full length fur coat, his eyes are wide open and he begins to notice that there's a big, wide wonderful world on the outside of the pouch, and so he decides to become adventurous and takes a little walk on mama's back, and that's all he does for the next six months. At the age of one year he's still a relatively helpless bundle of cuddliness, and continues to cling to his mother's back until he's almost as big as she is. Why leave home, the rent is paid, and mother loves him.

Now and then when it's lunchtime, the young koalas get mixed up, and are fed by other females. Nobody seems to mind who gets whose milk, which is mighty unusual among wild animals. Mighty unusual among domestic animals too. After the meal the little ones return to their own mothers. Not much of a babysitting problem in parts of Australia, is there? However, Papa Koala isn't much of a family man, he just wants to munch on his eucalyptus leaves, and when the young one climbs on his back, he gets mighty annoyed and cuffs the baby a soft cuff.

A koala is full-grown at the age of four years, and if all goes well he'll live to a nice ripe old age of twenty years. All he ever eats throughout his entire life is the leaf of the eucalyptus tree, and never has been known to take a drink of water! All the moisture he needs is contained in the leaves, but he has a very delicate constitution, and sometimes the change from one eucalyptus grove to another may prove fatal, which is why you rarely see this charming little animal in a zoo. He's not well known for outstanding intelligence, but at least he's smart enough not to have any commercial value, like some of his relatives such as the opossums, the wombats, the bandicoots, and the Tasmanian devil, and with relatives like that maybe he's content to be the sap of the family tree.

THE ARCTIC IS HIS REFRIGERATOR

Polar Bear

If you're going to hunt the polar bear with a club, just make sure that there are about fifty people in the club, because, to man, the polar bear is one of the most dangerous animals in the world.

Man does hunt the polar bear. For instance, the Eskimos have a use for every part of the animal, his hide for clothing, his flesh and bones for food and utensils, and his claws for jewelry. The real trick is bagging one. You see, the polar bear doesn't see man too often and as a result he's not afraid of him and so just looks at puny man as just another morsel on the menu. When hunger hits the great white giant he'll track a human being across the icy wastes the way he tracks any other game, and with a persistence that rivals lint on a blue serge suit. Once close enough to his prey, he charges ferociously and can kill quite easily by biting, rather than in the usual bear fashion of a swipe with a huge and powerful paw.

The scientific name of the polar bear is *Thalarctos,* which means "sea bear," and sea bear he is, swimming better than a porpoise in an olympic pool. He's been spotted as far out to sea as 200 miles, probably looking for his favorite tidbit, a seal or a walrus cub. He'll also eat caribou, foxes, birds, shellfish, or anything available in the arctic deep freeze. He doesn't even turn his nose up at just plain seaweed—after all, salads are tasty sometimes too.

Just as the ideal marriage is one in which the husband would rather play golf than eat, and the wife would rather play bridge than cook, the ideal coat of fur for a bear that lives in a frigid, snow wrapped region would be thick and white—and so it is. Sometimes the white, heavy fur is tinged with a little yellow from the bite of the brine, nonetheless, an effective camouflage. The polar bear is admirably designed for life in the cold. For instance, the bear's feet are covered with hair, including the bottoms, and that seems like a pretty good idea for an animal that has to walk on the ice most of the time. Even though massive and powerful, he's more streamlined than other bears, with a long and relatively slender neck and head, making for more efficient aquatic maneuvering. He can see better than most bears too, and has a sharp sense of smell. Nice characteristics to have working for you when seeking food during a lean season.

And here's something that's as strange as an Adam's apple on a barber pole. The scientific folk who are concerned with such things, have some difficulty in defining just what a bear is. Everyone seems to be able to recognize a bear, but anatomically they're nothing much more than a very large, tailless dog. Some dog! The male polar bear can stand 5 feet tall at the shoulder, get as long as 9 feet, and weigh up to 1,600 pounds. However, the average male is more apt to weigh closer to 900 pounds with the female around 700 pounds, which makes it kind of clear that the only time to pat a polar bear on the head----is when he's a rug!

BLACK BEARD THE BISON

Buffalo

Once upon a time there was a 200 pound sportscaster who went on a diet. He lost four pounds a week, and in just fifty weeks we were rid of him completely. And once upon a time there was a group of animals in North America that numbered upwards of sixty million, with one single herd of four million that covered an area twenty-five miles wide and fifty miles long, which makes it difficult to believe that we were almost completely free of these animals by the year 1900. In 1901 there were only 300 bedraggled specimens left, and I think they were looking for a place to hide. Of course, the beast we're talking about is the American bison, or if you prefer, the Plains buffalo.

By 1970, the great, bearded, shaggy creatures had made a comeback, and at last count numbered somewhere near the eighteen thousand mark, which is remarkable because they're kind of difficult to keep as a pet. We don't really need them for food, clothing, shelter, or heat, and milking a buffalo could be as exciting as being a weight guesser at an Octopus convention. The Plains Indians, however, did depend on this tremendous wild ox for their entire livelihood, and so did the early western settlers. When the seemingly endless herds disappeared, so did the poor Indians. It was poke and plumb time. When they poked their heads out of the tepee, they were plumb out of food, clothing, shelter, and wherewithal for heat.

From the chin of the male a big black beard hangs, while the rest of the body is covered by rich brown, dusty short hair. Sounds like a hippie, doesn't he? The most striking feature of this refugee from a nickel is his tremendous head and massive neck, that flows into powerful humped up shoulders; and a long, shaggy cape of thick hair that doesn't have a passport to get past the shoulders. He's got short, stumpy, sturdy horns that curve outward and then upward, and a mind that a mind reader would only charge half price to read. He's a dummy.

The average bull weighs close to 1,700 pounds and the average Mrs. Bull, goes for about 800 pounds, and just for the record, there was a bull that tipped the scales at 3,000 pounds. And that's a lot of bull to be running around looking for another bull to fight for the leadership of a herd. But fight they did, and still do during June and July, for as everyone knows June is the wedding season. If the battlers are evenly matched they can fight for as long as two days and two nights in succession; the winner gets his leadership and his harem of cows, and let the female liberation movement chew on that for a while.

The buffalo is one of the few animals to face a storm head-on. No matter how hard the winds whistle or the snow blows, the bison points his head into the wind because he has that great mane, that thick mat of shaggy hair for protection, while his other end is relatively unprotected and would get as cold as the seat of the last man on a short tobaggan.

Bush Baby

Winston Churchill once said, "Show me a man who doesn't laugh, and I'll show you a man whose shorts are too tight!" And show me a furry little animal with a soft bushy tail, big brown, bright and beautiful eyes that cannot move in their sockets, and I'll show you one of the most attractive, cuddly, and interesting animals in Africa----the bush baby.

It is strange that this bright eyed and bushy tailed mammal can't move its eyes in their sockets, but to compensate, old Mama Nature has fixed his neck so that he can turn his head almost one hundred and eighty degrees and look directly backward, which might be all right for watching two tennis matches at the same time, but a darned nuisance if you had to cheat on an exam.

There are several kinds of bush babies, all cute, and ranging from a healthy mouse-rat size to a sickly house-cat size. All live in the forests of Africa, sleep during the day, and hurry and scurry around for food at night, looking mainly for things vegetarian, but not turning down a peachy little bird's egg or a tasty little lizard if he should happen across one. While he looks and scurries, he utters haunting little baby-like cries, poignant and petulant. Because of this happy little hunting habit, so we're told, he gets the name *baby*.

Bush babies are not the most docile of animals and are actually a little cranky by nature. They've been known to fight among themselves, sometimes fighting to the death, although there are more reports of them being tamed and becoming charming little pets than there are of them fighting to the bitter end.

However, they must not fight too often, because there's a strange habit they have that's best described as being a "ball of bush babies." Apparently they love company when they sleep in the trees for they huddle together in groups of four or five, legs entwined, arms wrapped around each other, heads nestled against furry bodies and heads, making one great big ball. It wouldn't surprise me if they all wish they had a deodorant that would take the worry out of being close. Make a great plot for a Swedish movie, wouldn't it---?

If you visit a zoo, make sure you see a bush baby, and pay particular attention to his ears. They're like thin, hairless, flexible, nervous, silver-dollar sized pancakes, always twitching, turning, and tuning, moving independently, almost as though they had nothing to do with the rest of this strange little crier in the night.

Agile is hardly the word for this charming creature. He can practically fly through the trees, galloping like a fur-covered coconut from branch to branch, not only speedily, but in a straight line. No beginner's wheels for him! Even in the dim, dim light of the jungle he can jump with amazing accuracy, as much as twenty feet per leap. But like everything else today, he's got a gimmick. His toes are long and slender and they have puffy pads at the tips, sort of like tiny suction cups. He can even run up a tree without using his claws. Bet he'd make an A-number-1 pickpocket, too.

HE RULES THE RODENT ROOST

Capybara

There's a rodent down in South America that sometimes weighs more than 100 pounds, which makes him the largest rodent in the world. No one's ever found a larger rodent, and since there are about 6,400 kinds of rodents, our friend the capybara gets the furlined camembert as the king of the rodent family. He's got more relatives than you can find around a disputed will, and all share the same characteristics. They gnaw. Porcupines, beavers, prairie dogs, chipmunks, hamsters, squirrels, woodchucks, muskrats, gophers, marmots, lemmings, rats, mice, and all their kin, share the same habit. They gnaw. And that's what it's all about, Alfie, rodents are mammals that gnaw.

All rodents have front teeth shaped like chisels, both upper front and lower front, and since they're in constant use, it'd be a sad state of affairs if they ever lost those front teeth, or even if they became dull. They'd be out of business and might even have to apply for federal aid, but here's the secret. The incisors of a rodent continue to grow throughout their entire lifetime, never really wearing out; the more they gnaw, the more they grow. Wish I had a bank account like that.

And while the capybara is King Rodent, he's still hardly known outside of his native continent, South America. Full grown he can be twenty-one inches at the shoulder and measure close to four feet in length. How would you like a basement full of those? Actually, he looks like the economy size guinea pig, and his scientific name translates exactly into "water-hog." Hog he's not, but water he lives by, in, and around. He's timid and shy and seems to wear a constant worried look. Just the slightest sound of danger and into the water he goes. He's a pretty good swimmer and even if he couldn't make the Olympic team, he does very well, swimming great distances underwater. Of course

heading for the deep six doesn't do him too much good, for while he loses a couple of pursuers, namely the jaguar and the puma, he gains a couple more who are just as vicious and just as hungry, that is, the local crocodiles and the local human beings. Not only do the natives consider him a neat 100 pound blue plate special, but they also use his great teeth as peace beads.

If you should someday be tramping around in eastern South America and find a couple of capybaras giving you the soft, inquisitive eye, you can bet your bikini that there's water close by. Capybaras are completely happy in the tall grasses that grow along the river banks, because they love to swim and they love to eat water plants and grass, and then, almost human-like, these peace loving creatures love to lie quietly on the bank and bask in the warm sunshine. When they're pleased they make a strange, low, clicking sound—sort of like a mechanical cat purring.

Females usually have litters of eight or ten and it doesn't take long before they're of a formidable size, staying together even though almost full-grown. In captivity they attain the ripe old age of ten years, which no respectable insurance agent would guarantee in the wild. In captivity, they also become surprisingly tame and affectionate, and if you're the kind of person who can grow to like a 100 pound rat rubbing up against your leg, or leaping into your lap, you might like to make one a pet. Some curators at zoos have.

Considering the trouble that man has with rodents in most civilized areas, it's kind of fortunate that the capybara is such an easygoing, rather-run-than-fight kind of animal. Can you just imagine the trap you'd have to set for a 100 pound rat, to say nothing of the cost of a five pound slice of cheese for bait?

HOW'D YOU LIKE TO
BUY HIS SHOES?

Centipede and Millipede

What makes a sound that goes 999-clump, 999-clump, 999-clump? A thousand-legger with a wooden leg! Ho, ho, ho! Humorous, but not true because thousand-leggers don't have a thousand legs. Ah, but they have enough legs to make them mighty uncomfortable if they had athlete's foot. The bodies of these speedy crawlers, like most worms, are segmented, sometimes as many as eighty-five segments, and attached to each segment are two pairs of legs, and so if you're counting, they could have as many as 340 legs, which makes you kind of glad you don't have to buy shoes for the kids.

The centipede is a mighty close relative to the millipede, or thousand-legger, with some major differences. For instance, the centipede has half the number of legs as the millipede, and his diet is somewhat different. The centipede is called a flesh eater because he eats insects like flies, spiders, and mosquitoes, while his leggier cousin digs decaying vegetable matter that he usually finds in the dark, damp places where he spends most of his time.

The adult centipede's legs end in a sharp spear-like manner, with the first pair of legs modified to form poison claws. These paralyze worms and insects, and there seems to be some truth to the legend that they can sicken a full-grown man. They make me sick just looking at them, but that's another story. It's also said that when one of the bigger species takes a speedy stroll across the bare skin it leaves a big, red, painful welt as a result of the irritation caused by the poisonous claws. Centipedes are soft-bodied and long-legged, while millipedes are round, hard-shelled, and have short legs. Who cares, and who's got time to check that closely anyway?

If you should inadvertently surprise a thousand-legger he'll curl up into a tight little circle with his hard-shelled back open to attack, but at least his softer underside and his legs are protected. He's also got one of the best defenses against being eaten by an enemy. He just doesn't taste very good, and the reason he tastes like he looks, is a set of glands along his sides that are filled with a foul-tasting acid that also burns when it comes in contact with a predator's mouth. Something like a bride's first attempt at curried kumquats.

There are about 150 species of millipedes in North America, and close to 200 species of centipedes, and many a housewife has claimed that they all live in her basement. Actually, those found in the dampness of a basement are not only harmless, but also helpful since they eat the other household insects like cockroaches, that make folks squeamish and uncomfortable. Try and explain that to a wife.

Chinchilla

The world's best salesman is the man who can convince his wife that she looks fat in a fur coat—especially if that fur coat is chinchilla. There are records of doting and dotty husbands or lovers who've paid as much as $100,000 for a full length wrap, which automatically makes a woman the most valuable fur bearing creature on earth. And who would dispute that?

What makes caviar so expensive? Well, sir, you have to consider that it's a full year's work for the sturgeon. What makes chinchilla so expensive? Well, sir, it takes the lives of over 100 of these tiny animals to make just one coat. The poor little creatures are only about ten inches long, their tails only about five inches in length, and obviously some of them aren't going to measure up, so the furrier has to really match and mate before he comes up with a one hundred grand garment---and that's even better than Liberace's dinner jacket.

The chinchilla looks something like a wealthy squirrel, with a sort of a rabbit-like head, with round ears that are about two inches long. But the fur, ah, the fur! The softness of down, the delicacy of gossamer, the fullness of Raquel Welch, and the exquisite color of a pale blue-gray sky at dusk. The fur is actually deep and full and sometimes instead of the pale blue-gray, a rich silver-gray. The delicacy is hard to imagine. One single strand cannot be seen by the naked eye which means that it's finer than a stingy spider's silken web. The quality of the fur and the density makes it impossible for parasites to move in, so you know the chinchilla is clean. Not only that, but he has no body odor at all. Arrid, please take note.

About the only place in the world that the chinchilla lives in the wild is Chile. (So maybe the name should be "Chinchile?") He lives high in the mountains and moves with the speed of summer lightning over the rocks, especially at night when he's got the most get up and go. And since he runs among the rocks and sharp stones, he has some pretty good-sized pads at the end of each toe to protect his feet. He has no claws so can't dig or climb trees, but he just loves to get together with a bunch of other chinchillas and live in holes in the rocks. A chummy little devil, isn't he?

Constant hunting brought this charming little animal close to extinction, but back in 1923, eighteen worried little chinchillas were brought into the United States and the beginning of the chinchilla farm was here. There are many farms now, and the danger of extinction has passed. However they breed very slowly, only one litter of one to four babies a year. Nine years is the average life span of a chinchilla-----if nobody needs a coat.

LA CUCARACHA

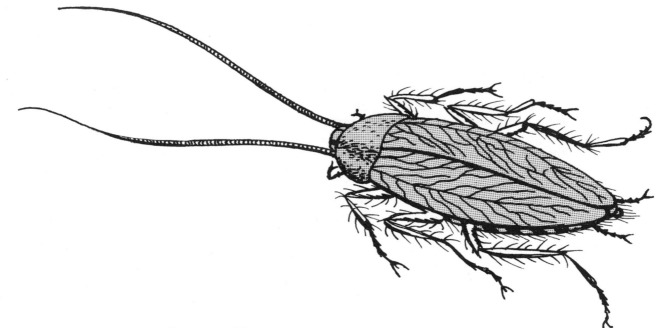

CHAS. HERZOG III

Cockroach

Way back in the dim dark past of creation, farther back than 350 million years ago, even before Madame Butterfly was a cocoon, there came into being one of the hardiest little creatures on earth. A scurrying six-legged little insect that was here when the Rockies were formed, when oil was turning to liquid in Texas, when coal was being pressed into existence in West Virginia, and 170 million years ago when the dinosaurs arrived, he was around to say howdy. You don't have to go to a zoo to see him, and odds are you couldn't be happier not to see him at all. We're talking about the lowly cockroach.

He's actually a living fossil, and has adapted better to more locales and climes than any other living creature. He can be found anywhere on the globe, in heat and cold, dry and wet, in burrows of squirrels, in the jungle, on the desert, in cash registers, television sets, and kitchens . . . you name it, he can live there. He'll eat anything from wax to orchid buds, devour shoes, and gobble glue that holds boxes together. He can survive on paint, loves soap, sips beer, relishes gravy spots on ties, can eat his own castoff skin, and can even digest wood, like his cousin, the termite. He can live a month without water or food, two months on water alone, five months on dry food without water, and never heard of Alka-Seltzer, but I'll bet he can eat it and gain weight.

Most folks think of cockroaches as filthy, but he's not really dirty. The thing that's misleading is his foul odor, because the cockroach has scent glands something like those of the skunk, that give him a nice fetid aroma, and at the same time a means of protection from his predators. Who wants to eat a smelly bug?

If you're planning on making a pet of a cockroach you've got many models to choose from. There are 3,500 known species, and only one percent of all the species prefers the home of man to other environments. Try and explain that to someone who's a got a kitchen full of speedy little night pests. Cockroaches come in a variety of sizes ranging from smaller than a grain of rice to as large as hummingbirds, with three inch bodies and seven inch wingspans. Yes, they can fly, but only when all other means of escape fail.

His most remarkable equipment is his antennae. Not only are they longer than his body, but they also contain olfactory organs that let him find his way in the dark to food and water, sort of long slender nostrils, you might say. He also uses his antennae to woo his lady love, stroking her antennae with his to excite her. From this meagre beginning springs love, and another million pests.

His hardiness rivals Superman. Step on him and his hard resilient body saves him; he skitters away when the pressure is relieved. Freeze him solid and he walks away when thawed—slowly, but nonetheless, he walks away. And any contortionist would be envious, because he can squeeze through cracks that seem impossible to get through. And if you don't think he's prolific, just consider the fact that the Russian Army once fumigated a barracks and collected 475,000 dead cockroaches from a single building! I'm sure sorry for the guy who had to count 'em!

Strangely enough, cockroaches are valuable in cancer and heart disease research and in nutrition studies, and even serve a useful purpose cleaning up dead vegetation that clogs our forests, but he's about as welcome as feathers in an omelette in the house. However, it's a pretty good bet that he'll be here long after we're gone, or, as we've often said, "Show me an arrogant insect------and I'll show you a cocky roach!

HE'S A RARE FISH

CHAS. HERZOG III

Coelacanth

These days most of us grow up knowing where babies come from. It's the birds and the bees we don't know anything about. And most of the scientists have grown up knowing that a strange fish called the *coelacanth* hasn't been around in over 150 million years. You see, the coelancanth is supposed to be the missing link between land and sea creatures and finding a living "link" would be like walking down Woodward Avenue and finding a *Tyranosaurus Rex* in a metermaid's uniform. But something almost as surprising happened.

Way back in the year 1938, off the coast of east Africa, a museum curator named Miss Latimer was checking the day's catch of sharks. One of the sharks didn't look like a shark, mostly because it wasn't a shark. It was a strange fish with fins that looked more like limbs than fins. Its scales were heavy and thick. It was five feet long and weighed 127 pounds with a big, ugly, underslung, and powerful jaw. Its color was steel-blue. Poor Miss Latimer didn't know what the heck it was, so she contacted a hip professor named J. L. B. Smith, an expert, teaching at a college in South Africa.

The professor took a deep breath, looked at the pictures, rubbed his eyes again and again, took another deep breath and identified the fish as a specimen that was thought to be extinct, unheard of in modern or even ancient times. Dr. Smith said it was the coelancanth, pronounced SEE-LA-KANTH, "the closest living relative of the long extinct fish that is accepted as the ancestor of all land animals.

He is almost in the direct line of man's ancestry." How many people have you met who looked like they had a fish face? (Editors excepted.)

The excitement in the scientific world was terrific. Rewards for additional specimens were offered, leaflets were distributed, fishing colonies were alerted, and the search was on. Since 1938, twenty-eight of these rare fishes have shown up, all caught between the months of September and February, at depths ranging between 650 feet and 2,000 feet. The biggest "living fossil" tipped the scales at 208 pounds and the smallest, at 43 pounds. They were all keepers, of course.

All the coelancanths were males, with one exception. A female was brought in alive in 1954, but died within four hours. She just couldn't stand the bright sunlight and gave up the ghost because she was too sensitive to strong light. (The opposite of television performers.)

The poor fish has, so far, demonstrated an extraordinary capacity for individual variety. In other words, no two of the twenty-eight were exactly alike. Some were blue, others green, some brown with white spots and phosphorescent eyes, and no two of them had their fins in exactly the same relative position. It's as though old Mama Nature was unraveling a mystery a little bit at a time, like the next clue comes in 50,000 years. Meanwhile, Dr. Smith keeps looking for additional specimens. And maybe he'll be lucky. After all, isn't this the Age of Aquariums?

Cormorant

Some people fish with worms. Some people fish with expensive gimmicks, lures, lines, rods, reels, poles, pins, weights, and wishes. And some people, believe it or not, fish with real live birds on a leash. In the Far East, India, China, and Japan, they capture the cormorant, a pretty good-sized duck-like bird, put a loose collar around his long neck, tie a line to the collar, go out in a boat late at night, light some torches or flares, and let the cormorant smell out the fish, dive into the water, and snap them up. Only trouble is, that with the collar on his neck, he can't swallow the poor fish, and all the fisherman has to do is drag the hapless helper back to the boat and pick his pocket, or rather burglarize his bill, and you'll have to admit that that beats baiting a hook.

The Far Eastern Izaak Waltons, if you want to call them that, usually have six or more cormorants per boat, and while one is fishing, they put hoods over the heads of the others, keeping them not only in the dark, but also very quiet. Wonder if that hood would work on children? Anyhow, catching the fish and not being able to swallow it must make the cormorant as frustrated as a bee on a paper flower, especially when you consider that he's been known for centuries as a symbol for greediness. The whole system is for the birds.

Fisherman have always felt that the cormorant was a dirty bird, not hygienically, but rather as an unfair opponent, and that he destroyed the good fishing spots because he had such a voracious appetite for fish. However, that's not quite true, because most of the fish he takes are worthless species as far as man is concerned.

There are twenty-nine species of cormorants, and most of them are black in color, with long necks and short wings, and about three feet in length. Their name originally meant "sea raven," mostly because they lived along the sea coasts, however, certain species also live on inland ponds, streams, and rivers, so maybe the name ought to be changed. They look a great deal like ducks and geese dipped in ink, and they fly in formation like ducks and geese, in loose waves and V's, with the only real difference being that now and then they stop flapping their wings and glide. Why work your feathers to a frazzle when you can coast now and then?

. The cormorant's long slender bill has a sharp hook on the end of it, the better to gaff you with, my dear, and often the bare skin of the face and throat is brightly hued. His feet are completely webbed, even the hind toes are included in the web, not free as on a duck, and he swims like a gold medal winner, sometimes using his wings, to ship around in a tight turn with the greatest of ease to run down and snag a finny victim.

Colonies of cormorants number in the thousands and they usually nest on the bare ground, although if there're trees around, they may take an apartment with a view, making their nests in the trees out of sticks. The eggs are bluish in color and are covered by a chalky chalk, hatching in about four weeks, with the little dark, ugly chicks screaming for food almost immediately. They're fed just like their relatives, the pelicans, by poking their beaks into momma's throat, and slurping up predigested little tidbits of fish and stuff, which can't be near as nice as pablum.

Cougar

They tell of the world famous philatelist who met Queen Elizabeth, but knowing her only from stamps, his first impulse was to lick the back of her head! And they tell of the cat fancier who met a cougar, but knowing him only from Walt Disney films, tried to photograph him and found him as elusive as smoke on a windy day. The cougar just doesn't like man. He likes to prowl around an abandoned camp or dwelling with great curiousity, all right, but just let a human being appear and faster than you can say "Felis Concolor" he's gone. Accounts of this cat's attacks upon humans are scarcer than bones in bananas. Man-killer, he isn't.

There are twenty-seven kinds of cougars, twenty-eight if you count the automotive one, and they have a variety of names, like: puma, panther, painter, catamount, and mountain lion, but whatever you call them, they're all lithe, long, lean, and powerful. It's rare that a cougar weighs more than 160 pounds when he's full grown, but there are records of this graceful cat having enormous power, strong enough to drag a 700 pound victim as much as 100 yards. What a pity he can't play fullback for the Detroit Lions.

The cougar's head is round and relatively small, and his eyes burn like hot ball bearings, but the most fearsome thing about this savage cat, so they say, is his wild, ear piercing shriek, a wild, weird, hairraising sound that makes you think of a hysterical woman whose purse is being snatched. If they could only duplicate that sound in an alarm clock I might get up on time.

This big cat is ferocious, make no mistake, whose natural prey are the deer and an occasional elk, but he's not above knocking off a smaller animal, like the skunk. And the thing that puts the cougar on the "wanted" list of the farmers and ranchers is his appetite for old-fashioned, easy to kill domestic stock, cattle, sheep, horses, and pigs, doing most of his hunting at night.

He can jump like a kangaroo with a hot foot, twenty feet in one gigantic leap, and seems to have no fear of height, being able to drop from a perch to the ground sixty feet below without hurting himself. Six feet of tawny, grayish-brown muscle with long murderous fangs. And he can swim almost as well as a seal in surf. More than once he's been seen swimming across rivers over a mile wide. No, he does not use the Australian crawl.

The cougar is found not only in the United States, but also in Mexico, British Columbia, and South America, where his natural and equally ferocious enemy lives, the jaguar. While the jaguar is larger and more powerful, it's no match for the cougar's agility in a fight, and it's an even money bet as to who walks away at the end of the fifteenth round, wagging his tail behind him.

At birth the cougar is about the size of a one-pound loaf of Wonder Bread, and grows stronger twelve ways—quickly. He opens his eyes on about the ninth day, cuts his first teeth about the twentieth day, loses the spots from his fine yellowish fur at about six months, leaves mama and the safety of home at about eighteen months, and lives an exciting, frustrating twenty years—if the brave hunters with yelping dogs let him.

HOLY COW
. . . SHE HAS FOUR COMPARTMENTS!

Cow

I think it was Orvilla Turnbull who once said, "Never milk a cow during a violent storm-----you may be left holding the bag!" And it was a research scientist named John Pallister who said that it was on Columbus's second voyage in 1493 that cattle were introduced to America, however, since folks didn't keep records so meticulously back in Chris's time, we have no written record of any of them stepping off onto Plymouth Rock, or whatever cattle step onto when debarking.

Anyhow, as far as man is concerned, there is no animal in the world as important as the cow or the ox or his relatives, for they have supplied and still supply him with food, clothing, shelter, sport, and occasionally a spate of literature such as the Gelett Burgess "Purple Cow . . . of which I'd rather see then be one."

The family name is *Bovidae* and includes not only cattle or oxen, but also sheep and goats, and the swift antelopes. They all have cloven hoofs, they're all cud-chewers, all have simple, unbranched horns that are hollow and never shed throughout the life of the animal. They always have a pair of horns, never a single, unless you believe in unicorns, in which case, consult your fable stable.

The question: Why does man climb mountains? The answer: Because it's there. And now the question: Why do ruminants chew cuds? The answer: Because it's not only a pleasant sensation, but also necessary for the health of the animal. For instance, the cow has four compartments in her stomach, not four complete stomachs, just four compartments, and they all have to be in working order to fill the udder compartment. We'll milk that line later on.

When cows eat grass or any other food, they only chew it long enough to swallow, at which point it goes into compartment one, where it's stored. Then it heads along the assembly line into compartment number two, where it's formed into little blobs or cuds. Then when Old Bossie is resting, she brings the cuds back up, urp, one by one, and chews the stuffings out of them, mixing them with saliva all the while. Now when the cud is swallowed for the second time it goes to the third compartment where the real work of digestion begins, finally making it into compartment number four for final disassembly. Can't you just imagine what a stomach ache on a cow would feel like, or what would happen if she ever got the hiccups when the cud was coming back from compartment number two?

The first part of the stomach is called the *rumen* and any animal with this tricky kind of digestive tract gets its name from that compartment . . . a ruminant. Ruminate on that for awhile. And while you're ruminating, you may like to have a useless piece of information that comes in handy when the conversation lags, such as: The world's record for the largest domestic ox is an animal that weighed over 2,800 pounds! And that's a lot of bull.

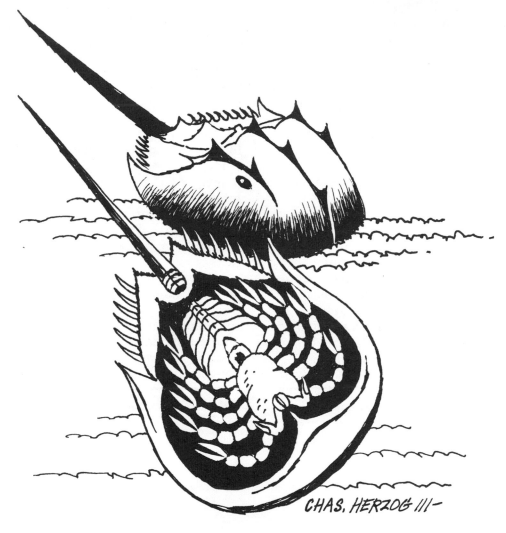

Horseshoe Crab

They say that if you plan your vacation right, you can be out of town when your relatives arrive. Maybe. But the horseshoe crab, a sea creature that looks like an army helmet with legs, really doesn't have to worry about relatives. He's in a class by himself. He's not really a crab, you see, The naturalists say that he belongs to an ancient group of animals that has survived over 190 million years with relatively little change either in living habits or body form. Nonetheless folks call them *crabs*, and of the five species around, four are mighty good eating, and go under the name of king crab.

One specie of these strange-looking creatures is found along the Atlantic coast from Maine all the way down to the Yucatan and isn't the edible one. The other four kinds are found in the East Indies and southern Japan and are the unlucky moneymakers gobbled up by gourmets.

Horseshoe crabs breathe by means of gills. They have compound eyes, five sets of walking or swimming legs, one pair of pinchers, no antennae, and a six inch tail spine. They average about twelve to fourteen inches across the back and sometimes grow as large as two feet across, which is why some folks call them "king crabs." And if you look down on them through shallow water they look hoof-shaped, which is why some folks call them "horseshoe crabs." In any event, from the top view they're brownish combat helmets, and from the bottom view they're as ugly a mess of legs,

abdomen, gill plates and stuff as you'll ever want to see. It'd give an Excedrin a headache.

The horseshoe crab literally runs along the sea bottom with an eerie sort of bobbing gait, each set of legs activating independently in a sort of wave-like motion, finishing off with the gill plates undulating last. With each beginning wave he nosedives into the sand and as the gill plates take over he tilts upwards. If he runs too fast he literally takes off with only his tail dragging. Sometimes he'll just swim upside down like a rusty tin soup bowl, finally settling to the bottom and turning himself over with his tail spine. It's a form of locomotion that seems as frustrating as driving home on a jammed freeway at 5 in the afternoon.

Each spring when time and tide are just right, horseshoe crabs climb up on the beach to lay their eggs in a shallow depression in the sand. When hatched they resemble the adults except they have no tails. The rest of the year they feed on mussels and marine worms. And here's the wildest thing about them---they have no jaws, yet they chew their food in a manner that would make most dentists rub their drills in glee. The mouth, if you want to call it that, is hidden between the bases of the five pair of legs, and as they move their legs, the mouths, or shoulders, just grind away, "chewing and chomping" as they move. Nifty, huh? I wonder what happens if they get bursitis in the shoulder joint? Probably have to invite a masseur to lunch.

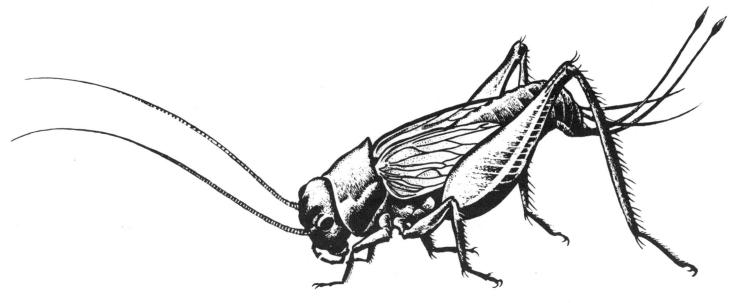

CHAS. HERZOG III

Cricket

He fiddles, he fights, he's an acrobat, a ventriloquist, and, best of all, he makes music that's friendly, unique, and reassuring. He's called a cricket, an insect that has ears near his front knees, and sings a strange clicking, chirping song, something like a minute electric typewriter with hiccups.

Way back in merrye olde Englande, a cricket in the house was supposed to bring good luck, until folks found out that a cricket will eat almost anything and makes a moth look like a rank amateur when it comes to leaving holes in clothing. He'll even eat leather. Outdoors he can chomp like a champ, gobbling fresh food, decayed food, or animal or vegetable food, drawing the line, it seems, only at mineral food, and I wouldn't bet on that either.

Just why does a cricket chirp? Well sir, scientists got out all their sophisticated gadgets, tape recorders, oscillators, superhetrodyne resistors, miracle magnifiers, and bifocals, and found that he sings just because he likes to. He also sneakily uses his crickety song to attract the sexy lady crickets as well. He never opens his little mouth to chirp. You see, each wing cover has a set of over 100 triangular ridges, like tiny teeth on a musical saw, and he makes the sound by drawing one delicate wing-edge across the other, sort of like an insect Isaac Stern.

Trying to find a cricket by his sound is as difficult as finding eyebrows on a canary, mostly because he has the ability to ventriloquize, that is, able to throw his sound out of the everywhere into the here, and back into the everywhere again. If you've ever tried to find a cricket in the house you'll know what I mean. Not only that, but temperature affects his song too. The colder it is, the lower the pitch, the slower the chirp. A scientist named Dolbear even worked out a formula to use in case you've lost your thermometer. Here's how it works: Count the number of chirps in fifteen seconds and add thirty-nine which automatically gives you the temperature in degrees Fahrenheit. Darned clever, these weather bugs.

And if you're a romantic reader and remember days of old when knights were bold and fought for their ladies fair, then you'll be pleased to know that friend cricket also jousts with rivals for the hands, or is it legs, of his lady fair. Not only does he fight vigorously, but he also wears a light, flexible suit of armor, a tough covering that shields his soft body and acts as a pretty good defensive device as he hops merrily about his crickety business. Maybe it's this protective covering, his wondrous ability to use his long jumping legs, his strong jaws, and his ability to throw his voice, that makes him feel safe enough to let anyone know that he's continually around, whether it's in a house, up a tree, under a rock, or beneath a burrow.

The ears of a cricket are uniquely placed near his front knees. Little drum-like things that vibrate to let the female know the male is nearby, and to let the male know that she knows that he knows she's nearby. Incidentally, the female never chirps, chortles, or chuckles; she can't make a sound . . . and most males are in favor of that, by Jiminy!

DON'T GO NEAR HIS WATER!

Crocodile

It's quite fashionable. Alligator shoes. Ah, but what size shoe does your alligator wear? And how do you know it's an alligator? How do you know it's not a crocodile? What's the difference? That's what I say: what's the difference, who cares?

But there is a difference. Many people use the terms indiscriminately. Actually, there are several kinds of these creatures, all of which may be called crocodilians, but a crocodile and an alligator are two entirely different animals.

The snout of the alligator is very broad from the eyes out to the tip, hardly tapering at all. The head of the crocodile has a triangular shape; the snout becomes progressively and distinctly narrower from the eyes to the nostrils . . . and if you're close enough to notice the difference, let's hope it's in a zoo.

The Nile crocodile sometimes reaches a length of over sixteen feet and a weight of over a ton. A reptile this large could easily dismember and swallow a full-grown man. Their teeth are made in such a manner that they cannot bite off a piece of anything, so they grab fiercely, clamp down tightly, then roll rapidly, literally tearing the victim limb from limb. Sort of sounds like a description of a teenage dance.

Sometimes, if they are near deep water, they'll merely tug the prey down to the bottom, where they patiently wait for the victim to drown. Very few animals can stay underwater as long as the crocodile. Not even Tarzan. They have a special watertight valve at the back of their mouth, enabling them to open the mouth underwater without water flooding down their gullet.

An unusual characteristic of the Nile crocodile is the difference just a few miles can make. For instance, in one part of the river he may be a consistent man-eater, raiding the local beaches and lunching with dreadful regularity. Many natives seem to accept this rather stoically. It's as much a part of their lives as the tax collector is a part of ours, and that seems to be a fair analogy.

A few miles up or down stream, where both crocodile and man are in just as plentiful supply, he may be completely peaceful in his relations with his human neighbors, and even children splash without danger in the croc-filled waters. As for me----I wouldn't get into a tub with a bar of soap shaped like a fish.

RAVENS ARE IN . . .
BUZZARDS ARE OUT!

Crow

Once upon a time an intrepid farmer put up a full-sized figure of Sonny Eliot instead of a scarecrow, in his cornfield. Not only did it frighten the crows away, but they brought back corn that they'd stolen two years earlier! Which immediately lets you know that the crow is a darned clever bird. Matter of fact, some naturalists consider the crow and his close cousin, the raven, the most resourceful and cleverest of all the 8,600 species of feathered creatures.

Intelligent and adaptable are words that seem to fit crows and ravens, for they have a knack for finding food where other birds can't even find a place to look. Crows eat a wild variety of things, from insects, small mice, rats, corn, farmyard eggs, all the way to young rabbits, so you can see why farmers love them with the same warmth that they love foxes in the henhouse. Crows are about as popular as a hernia at a weightlifter's convention.

Crows and ravens make pretty good pets, however, with some of them even able to speak a few words. The old farmer's tale that a crow's tongue has to be split before it can speak is as false as the legend that snakes can milk cows. But they are fond of pranks and have a sense of humor, or so it seems, as they pull clothespins off wash lines, and pick up shiny objects, like rings, glasses, and money, and hide them away.

Ordinarily you can tell if the winter is going to be mild or severe by observing whether the birds or the trailers start migrating south first, but it'd be a difficult chore with crows. They don't seem to migrate much at all. They just seem to worry through the winter eating pot luck from day to day, anything edible, animal or vegetable. Sometimes they get a little careless and then they supply a meal for the great horned owl, which aside from the nasty human animal, seems to be one of their very few enemies.

Crows don't walk too well, but they fly like the sky was invented for them, using their three foot wingspread to streak along in an unwavering straight line, which makes the phrase "as the crow flies" understandable. And where the crow flies, so do other members of his family, like the jays and the magpies, but the raven even flies in skies where jays, magpies, and crows don't. Ravens are found as far north as the Arctic regions, existing up there by a cleverness just short of phenomenal, with a diet that's even more startling than cousin Crow.

The raucous raven was famous for its dismal croaking voice and jet black plumage a long time before old Edgar Allan Poe immortalized him as a symbol of death and bad luck. Maybe Poe picked the raven as his dark symbol because he could be found munching contentedly on some dead animal, calmly croaking and making a gurgling sound, like a leaky xylophone, as he took off to soar to great heights. After all, how would a poem sound if the punch line was "quoth the buzzard, nevermore"? Ravens are in! Buzzards are out!

A DOG'S LIFE HAS CLASS

Canaan Dog

Aldous Huxley once said that to his dog, every man is Napoleon; hence the constant popularity of dogs. Ah, but don't make the mistake of treating your dogs like humans, or they'll treat you like dogs. Only dog owners and dog lovers can dispute those statements, but there must be some truth there, otherwise why would there be over twenty-four million domestic dogs in North America alone?

Man has trained, kept, and used dogs almost since time began, and most folks believe that he was the first animal domesticated, being bred for herding, racing, guarding, hunting, and even for means of transportation. And just recently a breed that was thought to have no use, was thought to be extinct, has started to make a comeback, the Canaan dog of Israel.

The Canaan is an unusual and interesting breed whose beginnings date way back to prebiblical times, with stories of Jezebel, the legendary queen, having one chained to her throne with solid links of gold, while the collar was not only gold, but encrusted with gems as well. Some dogs lead a dog's life with class!

Over two thousand years ago as ancient Israel disintegrated, the dogs began becoming scarce, after all, when survival is a form of existence, who can afford a pet? And so the Canaans began reverting to their wild state, slinking off the Negev desert to live as best they could on the harsh land. Some of the dogs retained a form of domestication through serving the Bedouins in guarding and herding, and until around 1934 that's been their history.

In 1934 Professor Rudolphine Menzel moved from Vienna to Palestine, and in 1935 she began trying to develop a breed that would suit the country and its problems. She remembered the Canaan and felt that any dog that was hardy enough and smart enough to live on a barren land for all those years must have a touch of courage and a little more than average intelligence. And so the wild dogs were collected, captured, and cataloged, and are beginning to make a comeback into the family of man. Nobody's too sure the dogs are happy about it.

In any event, these handsome canines are beating extinction today, because indeed they're proving to be highly intelligent, easily trainable and are serving as sentries, messengers, seeing-eye dogs, even land-mine detectors. They seem to love children, older people, and almost any climate. They don't seem to require too much care either . . . not much grooming, tail docking, or ear cropping. They even seem to enjoy living in apartments, which is a wonder all by itself.

The Canaan is collie-like in appearance with a coat similar to a German shepherd, and is the only breed of dog known to be related to the Basenji, the African barkless dog. They vary in color from the golden brown found on the sandy wastes of the desert, to the black and white and brown and white specimens found in the more densely populated northern sections of Israel. There are even brindled colored dogs and also some nearly solid black. Some for almost every taste. At last look there were about one hundred and fifty Canaans in the United States, and I'm told one of them owns his own "barking lot." Now that's what I call smart.

Daddy Longlegs

Abe Lincoln said that a man's legs were long enough if they reached the ground. And the same thing of course, applies to spiders, especially Daddy Longlegs, which, technically speaking isn't a spider, just an interesting close relative, who looks like a spider, walks like a spider and gives you that creepy feeling just like an eight-legged web spinner does.

But Daddy Longlegs isn't a spider. He flunks some of the qualifications, such as: his body isn't the right shape, it's round or oval with no pinched-in waist; he only has two eyes set up on a couple of short projections, instead of eight like most spiders do; he produces no poison at all; can't spin a web; doesn't bite; and doesn't make a nest of any sort.

In England, this ungainly little brown bodied creature is called the "Harvestman," in France he's dubbed "Les Faucheux" and in Latin his name is "Opilio," which means "shepherd," all names that suggest he has something to do with gardens or fields, and that's true. In early fall they're as commonplace as rice in a Chinese restaurant, scurrying everywhere, over the trees, down the fences, across the ground, to and fro, back and forth, here and there, from leaves to woodpiles, from house to barn. Farmers consider a good crop of Daddy Longlegs, an omen of a good crop, a good harvest, and a good profit, and as a result, it's considered bad luck to kill one----especially for the Daddy Longlegs.

He feeds on spiders (sorry about that, cousin),

mites, decaying matter, and is very happy with a piece of bread, a scrap of meat and a little fat. One thing, he's got to have, though, is a darned good supply of water; he may live without food for a time, but if water is in short supply, in no time at all he drops and dies, and kicking the bucket with eight legs is nothing to look forward to.

While this little bug bites no one, bothers no one, and destroys nothing, he does have one dinky little habit that could be disagreeable if you're the type that likes to handle creepy, crawly things. On the underside of his abdomen are a couple of glands that have the function of putting out a skunky, funky, smell. Sort of an underbody defensive odorant.

Just before an autumnal frost arrives, Mama Longlegs lays her eggs in some damp earth. The chill of winter snuffs out all the adult Longleg family, but the eggs, underground, stay fertile and fresh, and comes springtime, they hatch and start the cycle all over again. It's like painting the Golden Gate Bridge—it never ends.

The scientists, that hardy, informed group who watch such things, say that old Daddy Longlegs is the sexiest critter of them all, a regular Casanova. No courtship, no waste of time sending flowers, no dancing, no music, no candy, no nonsense. The boy and the girl get together, decide they were meant for each other, and that's it. The male sex, the female sex, equals insects---ain't life simple?

KOMODO THE SNEAKY DRAGON

CHAS. HERZOG III

Komodo Dragon

How do you hide on eighteen foot giraffe in a phone booth, or a twenty foot python in a picnic basket-----or a ten foot long lizard on an island? The first two are impossible, of course, but the truth of the matter is that there is a ten foot long animal that has existed for several million years but wasn't discovered until the year that Arizona was admitted to the Union.

In 1912 a man named P. A. Ouwens went exploring down among the islands of Indonesia and came across a lizard that was so large, so fearsome looking, so unknown, that he thought it was the mythical dragon that breathed fire and stole lovely maidens to sneak into his cave for a midnight snack. Of course, this animal was one of the species of lizards called a *Monitor*, a ponderous creature that grows up to ten feet in length and can weigh 100 pounds or more. And since it was on the island of Komodo, that he saw them, Mr. Ouwens simply called them Komodo dragons. See?

And don't think it was easy for old Mr. Ouwens to capture the first five specimens, because this giant lizard is a pretty sneaky character. Wary, to say the least. He lives in among bare rocks with bushes here and there and tall grass now and then, and bushes galore, so that as he sneaks and stalks, with his long, snakelike tongue constantly darting in and out, he's just darned hard to see. If you're ever on the island of Komodo, you'd have to build something like a duck blind and just develop patience, if you want to see one. It's easier to go out to the zoo, and safer too. You see, the "dragon" has many sharp teeth plus a thick strong tail capable of raising a pretty good welt as he lashes or thrashes.

It wasn't until 1926 that a scientific expedition went to really study these exciting lizards. They built a blind and put out the carcasses of some wild hogs as bait, and watched and filmed as the "dragons" clawed and ripped off huge chunks of meat, sometimes gulping down hooves, hide, hams, and backbone all in one swallow. Table manners he hasn't got. Normally, he doesn't feed on carrion, but on wild hogs and small deer that run free and unfettered on the island. The young are hatched from eggs that are laid in the ground and are born with yellowish bands on the tail and body. When they're full grown adults they turn a dull brownish gray.

Lizards are descendants of the same kind of animal that gave rise to dinosaurs, crocodilians, and birds, and the folks who study these things tell us that 60 million years ago the Komodo dragons had relatives living in Wyoming. If they had survived, maybe horses never would have been needed for transportation, and our pioneer ancestors might have traveled in "dragon" trains!

LOVES FISH, HATES FISHING

American Eagle

Did you know that we were only a wing-beat away from having the wild turkey as a national emblem? That's true. Old wily Benjamin Franklin wanted the turkey instead of the bald eagle. After all, considering the turkey's eggs, and delicious meat, you could eat it before it was born and after it was dead, a fitting symbol for a land of plenty. And besides, the habits of the bald eagle aren't nearly as heroic as you might think.

The great horned owl, much smaller, with a disposition like a woman scorned, sometimes just moves into an eagle's nest and without much trouble boots the "brave" eagle out. Of course, the eagle isn't really a patsy, although the great horned owl has his number. Baldy does his heaviest work when the osprey is flying around with a freshly caught fish in his talons. Then the dirty bird moves in, chases, wheels and whirls, worrying the osprey until he drops the fish, and it becomes a tasty snack for the bigger bird. Actually, the American eagle eats fish as his regular meal, even though he rarely can catch them himself. He soars effortlessly over the water looking, looking for dead fish in any condition at all, which he gulps down, burps, and continues to look. The eye of an eagle would make an optomistrist go out of business. He can see his prey, a dead whatever, at a distance of over three miles!

And don't worry about buying a toupee for a bald eagle, because he's not really bald at all—he just looks that way from a distance. I think he's kind of handsome in a bird-like sort of way, with his snow-white head and tail and dark brown body, standing over three feet tall on his tippy talons. His wingspread is over six feet, sometimes larger, and he really needs no slimming down, rarely weighing more than twelve pounds. And the story of this bird carrying off children is about as true as the one about finding newborn babies under cabbage leaves.

Unfortunately, the bald eagle is slowly becoming extinct, thanks to wild stories of his ferocity and the ignorance of some hunters. He's most plentiful at the two extremes of his range—Florida and Alaska, and is now protected by law. Now if we could only do the same for man.

The eagle's nest is a pretty sloppy affair, made up of sticks, lined with grasses and other softer items to make a more comfortable place for the young to hatch and grow up in, which is probably what makes the old man's head turn white as he reaches adulthood. The nest is lived in year after year, continually repaired until it becomes a monstrous thing of sticks and mud and dirt. There are records of eagles' nests weighing more than two thousand pounds! How'd you like to make bird's nest soup out of that? Ah, well, be it ever so humble . . . .

ZOOLOGISTS DIG WORMS THE MOST

Earthworm

One of the biggest laugh-getters in the happier days of vaudeville was the one about the worm who stuck his head out of the moist ground and seeing another worm immediately fell in love with it . . . at which point the other worm wriggled wryly and said, "Don't be silly, I'm your other end!"

Well, the head and tail may look enough alike to fool a worm, but if you'll look closely next time you see a writhing wriggler, you'll notice that the head end of the earthworm is pointed, the tail is flattened somewhat, which I'm sure will make a big difference next time you bait a hook. Worms are wondrous for fishing, all right, but they're even more talented and useful in the farms and gardens. Matter of fact, some zoologists call them "nature's plowmen." They dig them the most.

Aside from the ability of the earthworm to stretch or shrink incredibly, he has another trait that's almost as neat a feat, and that's his ability to crawl along and also climb some extra smooth and slick surfaces. He can do that because he has some teeny-weeny bristles on his underside into which he oozes a mucous secretion that makes him somewhat sticky and slimy at the same time, which is just what a poor fish likes----sort of like live spaghetti on a hook.

The wiggly worms in this country are usually reddish or pinkish and rarely get over ten inches long, but in parts of Australia there's an earthworm that grows to the astounding length of ten feet, and I'd love to see the early bird that gets that worm.

Probably have to be a vulture with Vic Tanny lessons, who has lots of pull.

The segmented body of the earthworm helps him squeeze and burrow, stretch and dig, until he has a comfortable underground lair to stay in during the day and to sneak out from at night, gliding silently in search of something to eat, like decaying material. Sometimes he drags his food below ground to chomp away at his leisure, and it's this dragging stuff below ground, eating, digesting, and coming back to the surface with dirt and digested material that makes this animal so valuable. Constantly plowing and pulverizing really makes the earthworm the farmer's friend.

Charles Darwin guessed that each acre of land contained as many as 50,000 worms, and in one year's time, these creepy, crawly things could help cultivation by turning over as much as fifteen tons of soil per acre. Maybe that's where the expression "one good worm deserves another" comes from.

Earthworms are hardy creatures and live in any part of the world where they can find slightly damp soil; however, too much water is almost as bad as not enough, and oftimes after a particularly heavy rainfall, you can see hundreds of them crawling up out of their burrows for air. It's this habit of coming to the surface during downpours, that gave rise to the superstition that the worms had "rained down." The truth of the matter is that they "rained up!" And that's what I call getting to the top . . . the hard way.

HAVE TRUNK, WILL TRAVEL

CHAS. HERZOG III

Elephant

Did you know that the elephant's trunk has 40,000 muscles, that an elephant has eyelashes five inches long, has a digestive system that rumbles so loudly that it can be heard a quarter-mile away, and that the only animal on the face of the earth that's larger and more powerful, is the big blue whale?

Let's start with that amazing, fantastic trunk. The scientists call is a *proboscis*, you can call it a *nose*. It's long, flexible, sensitive, and clever. With this trunk an elephant can pick up a lump of sugar, a peanut, or a straight pin, open automobile doors, blow the horn, untie complicated knots, unscrew light bulbs without breaking them, slam a lion to the ground, or tear a tree from the earth.

This mighty creature, contrary to belief, does not drink through his trunk; rather he sucks up about five gallons of water at a time and sprays it into his mouth, which may quench a big thirst, but doesn't do his sinuses any good. He does the same thing with dust, spraying it on his thick skin like talcum, and as Ogden Nash once said, "A little talcum is always walcum." And even though he has big, floppy ears, his hearing isn't the best, and his eyes are weak, and so once again the all-encompassing trunk comes into play. He tests the wind with it, checks out suspicious objects, and smells danger when it's near. There's even a report of this great beast throwing a full grown man over 120 feet. Imagine what he could do with a football!

An elephant's skin is over one inch thick, yet so sensitive that he can feel a mosquito landing on his hide; and he's so aware of cold that just the slightest frost will give him a real sense of discomfort. An eminent zoologist named Edmund Heller said that the only cure for this discomfort was a bucket of water laced liberally with gin, or rather a bucket of gin laced liberally with water and a smidgin of ginger. Two bucketfuls usually gets rid of the chill, but the wily pachyderm then fakes the aches and keep begging for another treatment, which in a short time could make him a candidate for EE, Elephants Enonymous. (Their color, of course, would be pink.)

These giant animals, like all mammals, have hair. It's short, bristly, and more like steel wires than hair. In captivity the hair is harmlessly trimmed with a blow torch. It's easier than shaving, and there's many a morning my face has felt the same.

The elephant's tusks are his incisors that continue to grow throughout his life. All his other teeth are molars—huge blocks that line each side of his upper and lower jaws—and if you're counting, he has twelve. He is strictly a vegetarian, eating as much as 500 pounds of fodder a day, in the wild. In captivity, he chomps up 150 pounds of hay, mixed with fruits and vegetables, but not too many oats, because elephants, like horses, "feel their oats." As one trainer in Ringling Bros. Circus said, "They'll eat everything but meat. They'll even eat sardines---if you leave them in the can." Please pass the Tums.

Asian elephants are smaller than African elephants, if you call nine to ten feet tall at the shoulder *small*, and they weigh 6,000 to 7,000 pounds, with the skin a little lighter in color and smoother than the African kind. The ears are much smaller too. The African elephant grows to a height of thirteen feet and can weigh over 12,000 pounds, while his ears grow up to four feet across and five feet long. The better to hear you with, my dear! The African sleeps standing up, never lies down, while the Indian elephant lays his bones down at siesta time. No one has ever found the mythical Elephants' graveyard, and no one has ever known an elephant to live past seventy years of age, and no one has ever seen an elephant with a sore toe----call a "toe truck!"

Archer Fish

I've been told that man has developed a gun that shoots bullets over a 100 miles and then throws rocks the rest of the way. And then there's the water pistol that shoots sand, for kids who live in the desert. But the strangest gun in the animal world is the concealed weapon that the Archer fish uses to mow down his meals.

This finny fink could be the super spy of the underwater world, because from the outside the Archer looks no different than thousands of other fish. Its body shape is characteristic, ranging between four and ten inches long, its snout doesn't seem to have any special gimmick for shooting, its mouth isn't overly large, and its eyes are not anything special, but when this aquatic Annie Oakley zeroes in on a hapless victim, well sir, an acute case of liquidation sets in.

Whoever named this fish must've been a fan of Robin Hood, because the drops of water it shoots are more like bullets than arrows. A careful look into the mouth of this insect killer shows how he conceals his weapon, and just how he loads and fires. Along the roof of the mouth is a narrow groove, the grooviest, and when the Archer fits his tongue along this groove he makes a thin, straight tube, sort of an animated peashooter. A gulp of water, a closing of the gill covers, and zappo! Another victim takes the deep six.

Up to a distance of four feet the Archer fish is deadly—never missing, and some of the larger specimens can shoot a watery bullet as far as twelve feet. And when you consider the problems this sharpshooter has to overcome to hit its target you just have to be impressed a little more than somewhat. The Archer cruises just below the surface of the water, spots his prey, manuevers into position, and sticks just his snout, nothing more, out of the water, and squirts off an aquatic "bullet." His eyes are still under water and so he has to compensate for distortion, refraction, current, ripples, and wind—pretty good for a watereyed, nearsighted sharpshooter who never heard of Samuel Colt.

This deadly little maritime marksman lives in the waters near the coast of southeastern Asia, from India to the Philippines, and doesn't really care if his victim, sitting so unconcernedly on a leaf or nearby bank, is a land insect or a water insect, he just salutes 'em, then shoots 'em.

THESE GUPPIES ARE GOLDPLATED

Goldfish

I've heard of the guy who had trouble with his owl because it said "How?" instead of "Who?". But how about the guy who had trouble with his goldfish because it kept tarnishing? Maybe he didn't know that goldfish don't retain their yellow-gold and red-gold color when they revert to the wild state. They just become dull, uninteresting, ordinary-looking kind of fish that eat anything that won't eat them first.

The wily Chinese, way back in the tenth century, were the first to domesticate these relatives of the carp, breeding them, crossbreeding them, and then crossbreeding them again to come up with specimens of almost every conceivable color combination, with and without fins, or tails, with oversized fins and tails, with bulbous eyes, with body shapes that looked like giant commas, even some that couldn't swim. About the only thing they couldn't develop were goldfish that had no gills.

Wild goldfish are naturally at home in southern China waters, and before they were made pets the Chinese used to eat them. Now that they're pets they still eat them. After all, why should they be any different than a pet clam? Along about the beginning of the sixteenth century the golden ones were brought to Japan, where the Japanese immediately improved on the design, produced them more cheaply, and within 200 years were exporting them to Europe. By the year 1790 goldfish bowls in Europe and England were as commonplace as sneezes in a snuff factory, and just sixty years later, the goldplated guppy made it to the United States, where it's now living the good life, at between fifteen and thirty cents apiece. However, selective breeding has produced strange, one-of-a-kind specimens that have sold for as much as $700. For that price, the gold ought to be real.

One of the reasons that goldfish don't get too large is that they're usually kept in small, confining bowls or aquariums, but if they have the room to spread out they can get up to two feet long, which could easily lead to a horror movie entitled *The Golden Gourmand That Ate the World!* Goldfish have been known to live to the ripe old age of twenty years or more, and since they don't make too much noise, and don't beg to be taken out at night, they make pleasant pets.

Mama Goldfish lays over 1,000 eggs at a time during spawning season, and if the water is around 60 degrees, they hatch in about 9 days. Just imagine, a 1,000 eggs at a time and no one ever remembers her on Mother's Day! Anyhow, ecologists say they should never be turned loose in domestic waters because they can too easily become pests, nuisances, and a threat to native fishes, as they stir up the bottom in search of any kind of soft animal or vegetable matter. Too bad these finny vacuum cleaners with scales can't eat beer cans or munch a bunch of mercury!

Flying Fish

Ever see a cigar box? Ever see a horse fly? Ever see a fish fly? Well, did you ever see a fish glide? You could have seen a fish glide, but fly, no . . . at least that's what the learned ones who study such things say. "Flying fish" do not really fly, although there are thousands of people from Miami to Mandalay who will swear they've seen this wondrous phenomenon. Way back in 1929, an experiment in a wind tunnel proved it just couldn't be done. But the gliding this remarkable fish does is almost as astounding.

This finny phenom actually has two sets of fins, a large set that can measure eighteen inches across, called the *pectorals*, and a smaller set a little lower on the body, called the *pelvics*. What really happens is that the tail churns at a tremendous speed, giving the fish a speed of close to forty miles an hour, at which time the wet "Red Baron" surfaces at an angle, the large pectoral "wings" are spread, and while the tail continues to vibrate like a windshield wiper gone berserk, he takes off and soars forty to fifty yards. At about twenty-five miles an hour he settles back into the water and starts his wild ride all over again, linking the glides over and over again, sometimes in sets of as many as ten. Do they ever fly United? No, just solo.

Like good pilots they take off into the wind, and there are even those scientists who say that they take advantage of wind currents, maneuvering and banking by adjusting their wings. On their consecutive glides they may be out of the water for over a half minute and travel over a quarter of a mile at an altitude of three to six feet above the water. And while they may be good gliders, their sense of direction needs a compass, or they need a good optometrist because there are many, many reports of their landing on decks, crashing into ships, and occasionally even winging through a porthole. Not only are they grounded, but oftimes eaten. You might say, from flying to frying!

The flying fish is dark blue on the top of the body, and mostly silvery on the underside, while the so-called wings, are a nice even battleship gray. They "fly" both day and night, and while they're darned good eating, they're also difficult to catch with a rod and reel. They don't seem to like ordinary bait. But they are caught by slinging a net over the side of the boat, and then turning on a bright light, which in turn seems to turn them on, and they head for the light like the poor moth to the flame, and faster than you can say "cleared for immediate take-off on runway H_2O" they become a "net" profit.

Just why the heck do they fly, anyhow? Why not swim like the other 25,000 species of fish? About the only answer seems to be that they take to the air to get away from their enemies, and not for the joy of doing an immelman or a loop. Dolphins dig them the most, and so do many kinds of sea birds, who like foot-long blue plate specials with fancy fins. Flying fish are sometimes found as far north as Massachusetts and Norway, but the large schools are found only in warm waters. Seeing a group of these scaly projectiles take off and gracefully sail over a hundred feet before splashing back into the water is a sight to excite the eye and please the earthbound. Still, they're technically not flying. I suppose if old Mama Nature had intended them to fly-----she'd have given them tickets!

HE HUSTLES
FOR MUSSELS

Flamingo

Show me a hydroelectric engineer and I'll show you another dam builder! Show me a bird with legs so skinny that they look like pool cues with feet, and a bill that looks like a miniature boomerang, with feathers that vary in color from powderpuff pink to beet borscht red, and I'll show you a *Phoenicopteriforme*, of, if you prefer, a flamingo.

There are six kinds of flamingoes and all of them have pretty much the same kind of look about them, four of the species living in the Western hemisphere and mostly in the tropics. There's one type that doesn't dig the sea-level life at all, but loves the mountain air and lives high in the Andes on lovely Lake Titicaca. As you might suspect, he's called the Andean flamingo.

These of a feather live together, fly together, flock together, and sometimes will number in the thousands as they stomp around on their beanpole legs in shallow bays and tidal swamps, constantly in search of some succulent shellfish, their favorite food. And they get their food the hard way, because in order to find a tasty tidbit they have to practically stand on their heads. The flamingo hangs his head downward, upside down, with his eyes looking back between his legs, and then scoops his bent bill into the mud and shallow water, scooping up a variety of things like mud and shallow water with a mussel or two hidden in the glob, then, thanks to the sieve-like arrangement in his bill he separates the wheat from the chaff, the Alka from the Seltzer, and the mud from the mussel, all the while making a slurping, sputtering sound like a sloppy soup eater eating clam chowder with a fork.

Flamingoes are in many ways similar to ducks and geese, and some of the similarities are that they can float pretty well, have the same nutty arrangement for sifting food through their bills, and molt all their wing quills at the same time, just like ducks, which made the flamingo a "sitting duck" for the happy hunters, until laws were passed to protect this beautifully colored wading bird and prevent their extinction. Otherwise, it would have been "Bye, Bye, Birdie" for keeps!

Mama Flamingo lays just one chalky white egg at a time in a nest mound that ranges from six inches high to eighteen inches high and is sort of conical in shape. The nests are placed pretty close together in shallow bays and mudwater flats with reports of sometimes as many as 2,000 nests crammed into a small area, and when the birds perch on these tiny towers, preening and incubating, it looks like something designed by Salvadore Dali the morning after a bout with a pink, limp olive.

At the end of the month, the little down-covered flamingo pecks his way into life and by the time he's full grown he'll be four to five feet tall, with red legs, a long snake-like neck that makes the flamingo not only graceful but bizarre, and a delightful pink color. Something like a stork with high blood pressure.

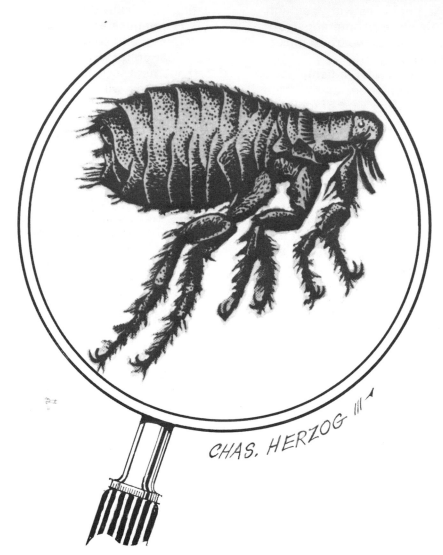

CHAS. HERZOG III

Flea

Pity poor Mama Flea . . . she knows that eventually all her children will go to the dogs. Which isn't quite true. As the saying goes, different strokes for different folks, and so it is with fleas. Different fleas like different food and as a result there are dog fleas, cat fleas, bird fleas, rodent fleas, rabbit fleas, chicken fleas, and there're even a few species of fleas who like smorgasbord.

Fleas (the adult ones, anyway) are bloodsuckers, and while they each tend to pick the host they were born to, they're not so snooty that they won't try something else. In other words, if they're not near the food they love, they'll love the food they're near. For instance, the dog fleas are happy on cats, rabbits, and rats, and if they can't start from scratch, they'll even jump on a passing human being and set up housekeeping.

And talk about jumping! In the insect world the flea is super, super flea indeed, and can jump hundreds of times his own length. If man had the same skill he could jump the length of a football field and never have to worry about a punt return. Fleas are as hard to see as salt in a sugar bowl, until you look at them under a magnifying glass, and then they show up as cunning little troublemakers with flat sides, stiff hairs, and too many sets of legs.

Freddie the Flea has no wings, which is why he has to jump, and the stiff hairs that cover his entire body all point to the rear, which makes it easy for him to slide forward, but scratching him back out is a rough go, while his flat sides let him slip unencumbered down to the skin without too much interference. He's usually a brick red-brown in color and his bite is much worse than his bark, for, as he sucks up the blood, he usually infects, leaving behind an itch that's bigger than an elephant's earache.

Strangely enough, the human flea doesn't thrive too well on the North American continent, although Europe seems to suit him quite adequately and so does the Eastern Hemisphere. Just why that is no one really seems to know, just chalk it up to the high cost of low life in America. He just can't get used to the fast pace, I guess.

There are mites, chiggers, and ticks, and while they are all easily confused with fleas, they don't belong to the same family. Their differences are many and minute and only the scientific sleuths really care. They all carry disease or discomfort or both, from the annoying and irritating itch right up to the bubonic plague that rat fleas give to man.

Then there are jiggers, fleas, or chigoes, which are not to be confused with mites, chiggers, or ticks. (Lots of variety in the flea market!) The male of the specie goes about eating in the usual fleazy manner, but the female, bless her, gets under your skin, lays her eggs there, and whips up sores that make ringworm look like a hickey by comparison. Just what good fleas do I'm hard pressed to find, but maybe it's as that old Confucian scholar once was heard to remark when asked why we have to put up with so many seemingly unnecessary irritations, "A reasonable number of fleas is good for a dog; it keeps him from brooding over being a dog!"

HE LEAVES DIRTY FOOTPRINTS

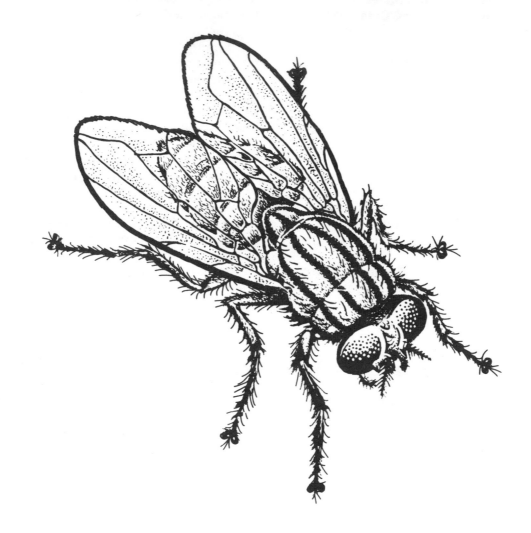

Fly

The only things certain in this world are death, taxes, and a word from the sponsor, to which we can add one more . . . a formidable enemy called the *fly*. To ignore the common housefly is to court misery; to neglect pest control is to pay for it with typhoid, cholera, anthrax, and summer dysentery in babies. Why, of why, didn't Noah swat 'em both when he had the chance?

The housefly starts out as a tiny egg, about the size of a puny pinhead, and within ten days it moves from egg to grub to adult, with a life expectancy of eight to ten weeks or about ten weeks too long. As soon as it becomes an adult it's ready to lay eggs, about 100 every nine or ten days, so that if you left a couple of lovers alone, and their offspring alone, and all the offspring lived, and were left alone, and you gave them four months to keep repeating this cycle, we'd be up to our navels in flies or about 191,010,000,000,000,000,000 flies!

The fly, a close relative of the dreaded tsetse fly, has only one real pleasure in life and that's eating, with an appetite that won't quit and a choice of food that knows no bounds, ranging from any dirty refuse pile to the sugar on your dinner table, spreading germs with glee and reckless abandon. And he's admirably equipped to collect germs and distribute them even without a zip code number. His entire body is covered with hair, including legs and feet, with an even stickier hairy pad on the bottom of his feet, which lets him not only pick up a few choice tidbits from the garbage heaps, but also allows him to nimbly walk the ceilings upside down, leaving the dirtiest and most dangerous footprints in the world.

You might think that the fly suffers from indigestion since he has no chewing mechanism, no teeth at all. The kind of fly that bites you is another variety called *tabanids*. The housefly just has big, soggy lips at the end of his nose, and, if you promise not to stop reading, I'll tell you just how he eats. For instance, to slurp up some sugar he has to soften it up and he does this by regurgitating a drop of fluid from his last meal . . . and all you thought he was doing was strolling joyfully around your sugar bowl!

Flies love to travel and tests have shown that a twenty mile trip isn't too uncommon, and in twenty miles it's relatively easy for him to pick up enough bacteria to make Louis Pasteur spin like a demented dynamo. Careful study has shown that a single housefly could have as many as five million bacteria on its hairy body. No wonder flies are as popular as an ingrown nose would be on a swordfish.

Most of the fly's head is taken up by his eyes. Thousands of tiny six-sided organs, each one a complete eye in itself and the total scene seen by a fly is composed of what the individual eye sees . . . see? One thing the fly doesn't need is fly-specs. This unsanitary little insect can be controlled and should be. For instance, protect spiders, the housefly's most effective enemy, and don't reduce the number of toads, lizards, and salamanders. Most of all, we ought to give them the bird, or rather give them to the birds such as swallows and swifts. I look forward to the day when we finally get down to the last miserable housefly and he lands near me when I'm armed with a brand new fly swatter, which at this point seems as remotely realistic as giving someone a $5,000 Persian rug . . . and a puppy.

HERE'S A FOXY LITTLE CRITTER

CHAS. HERZOG III

Fox

"Hey," said Turkey Lurkey to Chicken Little, "which came first, the chicken or Colonel Sanders?" "That sounds like something the sly, cunning, clever, speedy, Foxy Loxy might say," replied Chicken Little. And it's true, for indeed, the fox is sly, cunning, clever, speedy, and plentiful. There are at least eighteen different kinds of foxes living in America, Europe, Asia, the Arctic, and North Africa, and all of them, it seems, have the same problem . . . men love to hunt them for sport, for fur, or just because they dig the henhouse.

Foxes belong to the wild dog family and in the tradition of wild dogs, the fox is a fine father. He'll provide the food, stand guard against marauders, and if an enemy gets close to the family, he'll do his best to attract its attention, then lead the prowler a merry chase away from the den, oftimes putting his life on the line for his young. Not only a good papa, but also a fine husband, in his fashion. He'll live with his mate for the entire breeding season, and the family doesn't break up until the young are old enough to get out into the cool, cruel world and make it on their own.

Foxes are known for their big ears (the better to hear you with, my dear), but the ears on the little fox pictured cops the fur-lined hearing aid for the biggest ears on the smallest animal. This is the Fennec fox, a buff-colored little creature that measures only sixteen inches from the tip of his pointed head to the tip of his bushy tail, and his ears alone are the length of one quarter of his body, four inches long. He lives on the great, silent Sahara desert, where summertime or wintertime, the living's not easy. He'll dine on almost anything that won't dine on him first--insects, grass, mice, sugar and spice or a spare puppy dog's tail, if it's handy.

Oscar Wilde once said that fox hunting is nothing more than the pursuit of the inedible by the unspeakable, and I'm inclined to agree. One of the reasons for hunting Monsieur Reynard is that he runs a heckuva hunt. The red fox, for instance, will lope along at about five miles an hour, then suddenly spurt to forty-five miles an hour for a mile or so, then he'll backtrack, sidestep, head in another direction. Sometimes he'll run along the top of a fence or rail, scamper through the water to make the hounds howl, cross ice just thick enough to support his weight, while the unwary pack breaks through for an uncomfortable bath. He's a master at being elusive. One on one he wins. One against horses, man and dog, he comes in second best, even when he tries harder. Too bad.

I've heard of truck farming but never saw a truck grow, heard of rock gardens, but never saw a rock blossom, and now I'm told of fox farming, which seems like a bizarre way to run a farm. It all started back in 1894 in the Gulf of St. Lawrence, where silver foxes were nested and nurtured so that they could raise a family and care for them happily, only to be calmly killed and skillfully skinned so that some fashionable femme could become a fur bearing animal. It's a strange world, and so are the animals in it, especially man.

HE TAKES HIS TIME GROWING AND CROAKING

Bullfrog

The young folks have whipped up a new dance called the "Tadpole" . . . You wiggle your tail, turn green, and croak! And while you're clucking your tongue, shaking your head, and holding back a reluctant smile, let me tell you that that's just about what a real, live tadpole does. He wiggles his tail, turns green, and croaks.

Bullfrog tadpoles apparently are in no hurry to grow up into the harsh, cruel world of reality, because bullfrog tadpoles sometimes take close to three years to metamorphose. (Love that word.) Their legs don't even begin to look like legs until their second year, at which time the tender tadpole might be over six inches long. About the middle of his second year of life, the tail begins being absorbed, and by the end of the third year, the tail is gone, the legs are kicking, the color is green, and the whole bullfrog jumps out of the water to live on land awhile, at which time he measures two inches in length. In a very few short years, however, he can get up to seven inches long, and his wife eight inches long. And that's a lot of bull--------frog.

The American bullfrog is the largest tailless amphibian in the United States. The only frog that's larger is the giant frog of the Cameroons in Africa, which grows up to a foot in length, weighs as much as a fat cat, and can be caught only when the water is low. The "bee-deep" croak must be louder than the cry of a nudist baritone backing into a cold doorknob.

The law of the jungle may be eat or be eaten—but it's no different in the frogpond. The great green amphibian as a youngster eats insects, and when he's grown up, he'll eat anything that's small enough to get into his mouth. He'll eat all the crayfish he can catch, underwater, and on land he'll dine on a delectable diet of mice, birds he can catch, salamanders, toads, and even small turtles. He's not too particular about gobbling up some of his own kind if he can overpower them. Cannibalistic is the word. It's a tough world when, after a family dinner, you have to count the kids.

The other side of the coin, however, is just as devastating. The tadpole is killed by the giant water bug, which uses his hypodermic snout to suck the body fluids of life from it. Fish eat the larvae, and littler frogs and larger birds eat whatever they can swallow, but the greatest enemy is still man. It's hard to believe that close to three quarters of a million pounds of frog legs were sold in Louisiana alone . . . in just one year. Next time order pork chops.

Frogs of all kinds are found on all continents, with the northern half of the world having much more than the southern half. Twenty different kinds live in the United States, six species hop around Mexico, not counting the man with the "frog in his throat." And there's no truth to the myth that frogs or toads cause warts. But toads and frogs are closely related, kissin' cousins, you might say. The toad has rough, moist skin, while the frog's skin is smooth, slippery with mucus, and feels like a peeled, well greased, banana. So the next time you hear that an intrepid scientist has crossed a frog with a bunny to get Easter eggs with warts, smile, but don't believe it. Then there's the wart hog, but we'll save that for another book on animals.

HE BUILT A PEOPLE TRAP

Gerbil

Easy now, smile slowly, and don't groan too loudly as we recall the mouse who ran away from home because he found out his father was a rat! (You were warned.) Of course, there was no need to do that, for rats are quite fashionable now . . . not the kind of rat that makes a basement a dungeon, but a small mammal you might run across if you were hotfooting it across the sandy wastes of Asia or Africa. More and more folks in America are making pets of this desert rat. Naturally, they're not called rats, they're called gerbils, but it's still a rat no matter how you spell it.

Gerbils come in different sizes and several varieties, with the most popular being the ones about the size of a nice friendly house rat. The largest of the species has the colorful name *Rhombomys,* and makes his home in central Asia, around the Caspian Sea, or in Mongolia, and for an animal that lives in such warm climes to have such a thick coat of fur, which he has, is as surprising as hearing Dean Martin come out in favor of buttermilk.

Like most creatures that live in the still, still desert, the gerbil has large, large ears making it easy to hear sounds from afar, and even easier to hear sounds from anear. The sort of sandy, brownish fur is fine camouflage for living in sandy, brownish regions, which is precisely what they do.

The hind legs of this jumpy little animal are uncommonly long, and so, instead of being able to run and romp, scamper and scurry, like most rats, they sort of hop, hop, hooray in an almost-kangaroo style, and some folks, noticing the manner in which they move, call these gerbils "antelope rats." Other folks seeing them jump and gyrate say that they remind them of jerboas, or jumping rodents, and why not—"gerbil" is just nother way to say "jerboa." If you're confused, how do you think I feel? That's right. Jumpy.

These friendly little pets, when they live in their natural surroundings, burrow into the sand and call it home. Sometimes their charming little one-room apartments are connected to other little one-room apartments by a system of community tunnels, and while this seems fairly chummy, it's interesting to note that the male and the female usually do not nest together, and maybe that's really the secret to a happy marriage.

Most gerbils are active only during daylight hours, and when they're not chasing themselves around in high spirited play, they're on the lookout for seeds, roots, and grasses from which they get most of the moisture they need for survival, and don't let anyone tell you different—rodents will survive where angels fear to tread. They're hardy, they're helpful, sometimes they're harmful, sometimes. They also made it possible for us to have the Pied Piper of Hamlin teach us a valuable lesson; made possible Disneyland, the largest people-trap ever built by a mouse; and made it possible to have a word that you can use when you're tired of the four letter variety. A word with a little class, a little dignity, and a lot of uses. Of course, I'm talking about *ratphinque.* That's the French spelling, Monsieur.

Giraffe

There's nothing so stirring to the older generation than the sight of a graduating senior with his arms full of books, his eyes full of hope, his head full of knowledge, and his mouth full of bubblegum. And there's nothing so stirring to any generation than a herd of giraffes on the African veld moving at a full 35 mph gallop along the skyline. For animals that look so ungainly when spraddling for a drink of water, it's amazing the amount of grace and rhythm of action they have when running at full tilt.

The only thing living on earth that's taller than a giraffe is a tree—or maybe a basketball center. Some of these king-sized creatures become nineteen foot skyscrapers, which is higher than an elephant's eye, and a full grown man can actually stand upright between a giraffe's front legs—a not recommended standing place since a bull giraffe can weigh as much as 4,000 pounds.

The giraffe can't swim at all, but he sure can wade like the devil. However, you'll rarely see this long necked horse-on-stilts near the water, because only solid ground will support this huge, tall body. Dry, arid, firm and hard packed ground is essential, since mud or swampy country will bog him down and hopelessly trap him-----and he'd have a mighty hard time yelling for help since his vocal chords are as puny as an angleworm's anger.

And believe it or belittle it, but a giraffe actually does have vocal chords, although the sound they get from them isn't much louder than a clamoring clam's, and there are many who will say that they're actually mute, but apparently that's not true. There is one instance of a calf giraffe being ridden down on horseback, and the calf "blared" like a steer, and there's evidence that Mama Giraffe will occasionally make a low, soft sighing sound when her calf gets a little out of bounds. Now if they could only equip the Rock and Rollers of the world with the same kind of vocal chords, it'd make a great many of us as happy as a waterlogged walrus with waterproof moustache wax.

THE CANNY CANADA GANDER

Canada Goose

They say that everything is regulated these days. Even the Bluebird of Happiness has to file a flight plan! If you were to read the flight plan of the Canada goose, you'd find that the craft weighs about twelve pounds on the average, is thirty-eight inches long, and has a wingspread of close to six feet. It runs on grain power and the migratory schedule is so regular that you can almost set your calendar to winter when the Canada goose starts his jaunt to the south.

The Canada goose flies the friendly skies at a pretty good clip, too, flapping along at a steady fifty-five miles an hour. They travel several hundred miles a day, led by a wily old gander, who flies the point position of the V-shaped formation. Truly, beauty in motion! And don't think you won't know it when they fly over, because they "honk" a pretty good "honk" to let you know they're passing, whether it's day or night. I guess they have to honk—after all, they don't have turn signals!

Sportsmen consider the Canada goose number-one on their hit parade because he's the smartest of all the wild geese, cunning and careful—also shy and suspicious. You can add clever, too, clever enough to stay away from man or his sneaky "duck blinds." In other words he keeps his distance, which is considerable, but not necessarily enough.

In case you get close enough without a gun in your hand to take a look at the canny Canada gander, you'll notice that he's a conservative dresser, going in big for blacks and greys; his top half is grayish black, his bottom half, a grayish white, with a black neck and head and white cheeks. Drab and docile looking indeed, but don't push him too far, because he can give a pretty good account of himself, loudly hissing while he strikes strongly with his bill and wallops wildly with his wings.

While the Canada goose falls into the footloose and fancy free department, a peek into history shows that geese were domesticated many, many centuries ago. You can even find them on monuments in ancient Egypt; the Romans way back 400 years B.C. employed geese as "watchdogs," in a manner of speaking, using their "honk" as an alarm to let them know they were being invaded by the Gauls, or some second-story cat burgler. Ah, the goose hung high in the old days, whatever that means.

Geese mate for life, and if they're lucky enough to stay away from hunters, both two-legged and four-legged, they can live to a ripe old age of thirty years or more. And while it's still difficult to find a goose that lays a golden egg, it's not too hard to find one that lays four to six unspotted, normal eggs at a time, usually in June. Mama and papa and the little goslings all stay together during migration and the following winter. When spring comes, the older birds drive the young away to let them make their own mistakes. So how come they're called silly geese?

VIRILE THOUGH VEGETARIAN

Gorilla

Parents of teenagers soon discover that youth is stranger than fiction! True. And readers of fiction, especially Edgar Rice Burroughs's fiction, find that truth is much stranger than Tarzan ever dreamed . . . For instance, the great apes that raised Tarzan (on gorilla milk, whee!) are really docile, intelligent, vegetarians who live a dull existence, liking nothing better than to be left alone. And that sounds like a description of the average American father if I've ever heard one.

Several scientists have recently studied the habits of gorillas and found that many of the early mistaken ideas about them were as far from the truth as a politician's promise. It was thought, that the gorilla was a villain, with an open season on the dismemberment of man, that he fed chiefly on meat, and that when a large animal was killed that they hold a tribal dance with the females squatting in a circle to beat upon an earthen drum as the males danced themselves into a frenzy and roared challenges to the moon. All a bunch of malarky. That's more of a description of a college pep rally before a panty raid, than it is of a gorilla's personality. The truth is that the fearsome looking gorilla feeds on vegetation only, is an introverted, self-reliant, peaceful animal that lives to eat, sleep and belch, and keep the family group of twenty to thirty gorillas happy, safe, and not overdrawn at the bank. (Branch office, of course.)

With their huge heads, tremendous size, and ear-splitting roars they've built up a reputation that's bone chilling and completely undeserved, although early reports by African explorers said that the most manlike of all primates occasionally did attack man, but that the attacks were rare indeed. However, it does occasionally happen—and it's not a habit forming experience. Gorillas are incredibly strong. Captive gorillas have been known to bend or break tempered steel bars as thick as two inches, and there are several records of gorillas pulling guns out of the hands of hunters and literally tying their barrels into knots—and that includes the hunter as well.

Apparently, the gorilla is a bluffer, and rarely fights, but when he is threatened, he puts on a display that makes a South American revolution look like the rest period in a kindergarten. He rises to his six foot height, beats his tremendous fists on his kettle drum chest, roars like a jet plane in torment, lunges and thumps the ground with all the weight of his 500 pound frame. It's a savage display and usually intimidates the intruders. And that sounds reasonable.

Where does a 500 pound gorilla sleep? Anywhere he darn well pleases! But usually in a nest. They make crude "nests" in the trees or on the ground, lacing some branches together and adding a few leaves and forming a rough circle. The nests in the trees are necessary to keep them from falling out, but apparently the ones on the ground are built simply out of habit. Actually, because of their awesome size they live more on the ground than in the trees.

The leader of the family is called a "silverback" because of the silver hairs that cover his back and shoulders, and he's as undisputed as a shark in a swimming meet. He keeps order by staring intently with furrowed brow, keeping juveniles in line with light but effective cuffs, and roaring fiercely at all strangers, attacking only when necessary. Sound like your sixth grade teacher? Of course.

And so you see, King Kong was really misunderstood after all . . . he'd have come down from the top of that building and traded that squealing female for a truckload of celery. And in some instances that wouldn't be a bad trade at all.

CRUNCHY DELICACY

Grasshopper

There's an old line that says you can lead a horse to water---but remember what a wet horse smells like! And there's another old line that says that summertime is the best time for the sexes . . . the female sex, the male sex, and the insects! One of the insects we're concerned with is the familiar grasshopper, a jumpy little creature with short antennae, and a long history.

There are many, many species of grasshoppers in the United States, and most of them like dry, warm weather as they hop hither, thither and yon along highways and byways, near streams and fields, blithely chomping away on grass, which they like best, and any other kind of vegetation when grass is in short supply. Some grasshoppers prefer to live in forests, but they're the snobbish ones; they like the high-rise, high rent, trees with a view, where the food is plentiful and "leafing" is easy.

Strangely enough there are some grasshoppers that have no wings at all, some that have wings that are just decorative, merely pads, and completely useless in flight, and some whose wings carry them from place to place in a hurried flurry of activity. However, they all have hind legs that are perfectly developed for hopping, thick in the thigh and trim in the foreleg.

Gadabout grasshoppers are pretty active during the daylight hours, folding their tents, or rather their wings, at night and sleeping off the worries of the day, probably all worn out from rubbing the thick part of their leg across the edges of their straight wings to produce that dry-sounding, grasshoppery noise that's enchanting to another grasshopper, but a pain in the ear to most everyone else.

The truth of the matter is that the scratchy call is merely a love song that attracts the female who's thinking more of passion than pension and goes to the male with the loudest noise and the nicest looking legs. And if you think that's odd, just consider the fact that it's the male who screeches louder than the female for a change.

Another little item that's pretty strange too, is the placement of the ears. They're at the base of the abdomen, just under the wings, and look like two little, round, membranous tom-toms. I'd like to see the kind of earrings they'd have to wear on those ears, probably have to hold them on with a girdle and garters.

The family name of the grasshoppers is *Locustidae*, and when conditions are favorable, great numbers of these voracious insects will develop, gobble up all the nearby food, join forces with great numbers of other cousins, start using their family name, and become known as locusts. They start migrating, invading, blackening the skies as they spill from field to field, eating everything in sight and in nothing flat become known as a plague of locusts.

In some countries these migrations occur on schedule, and the natives, to make up for the loss of crops, gather in the grasshoppers instead, pull off the wings and legs, dry them in the sun, and store them as food for later on. And I thought the wings were the best part! And if that thought is making you twitch slightly, just consider that sometimes they eat the locusts alive by holding the (ugh) delicacy by the hind legs, ignoring the wings, and biting off the wriggly body. Now there's snap, crackle, and pop for you!

HUNGRY HERBIVOROUS HIBERNATOR

CHAS. HERZOG III

Groundhog

How much ground could a groundhog grind if a groundhog could grind ground? Or if you'd rather . . . how much marm could a marmot marm if a marmot could marm marm? Which is getting around to the woodchuck the hard way for, you see, the groundhog, marmot, and woodchuck are all one and the same, only the name has been changed to protect the weatherman on February 2.

Rip Van Winkle didn't need Sominex and neither does the groundhog. Every fall, just before the autumn weather reaches the goose pimple state, the chubby groundhog pussyfoots into his charming little chamber, sets his alarm clock for half past April, and settles down for his long winter snooze. His breathing slows down to a simmering sigh, his body temperature sinks to around forty-nine degrees, he curls up with a couple of mighty good friends, and that's all we hear from Gary Groundhog until old Sol, the happy sun, warms the earth in the spring. The legend that he wakes to see his shadow and predict a longer winter makes about as much sense as pushing a car uphill with a rope.

It's strange that even though the groundhog loves warmth, he's never found south of the Equator, never found in tropical countries, and never throws another log on the fire. You can see him in most parts of the United States and Canada, but only during the daylight hours and of course, mostly during the summer months. Woodchucks are lazy little devils, too, moving about in a leisurely manner in the late morning (not too early), filling up on clover, tender grasses, and other green goodies until the little belly bulges. When the sun hangs high, he just stretches out in a cool, shady place until the sun starts sinking slowly and the shadows get

long, and then he starts eating again till dark. Since there are no X-rated woodchuck movies to go to, all he can do is hit the sack and start all over again tomorrow morning. Ah, it's a tough life, if you don't week-end!

Actually, the marmot, groundhog, or woodchuck is more correctly known as a ground-dwelling squirrel, a rodent, if you will, and a close relative of Mickey the Mouse. The animal is sort of large, and heavy bodied, and while he's a little too large and lazy to climb trees with any facility, he will on occasion, scramble up a trunk, but rarely past the first fork. When full grown, this four-legged, furry barometer will weigh about nine pounds, and just before he hits the hibernation trail, he can weigh around fifteen pounds. After all, if you're going to sleep five months straight, it's smarter to have a larder.

And, you talk about the high cost of low life, well sir, just consider our marmot friend. At hardly any expense at all he builds a charming little apartment underground. One big master bedroom and several little side rooms. He even uses one for a bathroom when the weather is too weary for going outside, a fastidious creature, indeed. His burrow, or den, has a "front door" with a pile of dirt at the opening, a "back door" that's hidden so that he has an emergency exit in case a bill collector calls unexpectedly, and a third opening called a "drop hole" where he can calmly sit and watch the world go by. If danger threatens, he just drops out of sight, suddenly, straight down the shaft about two feet, to safety below. Which is known as giving your enemy the shaft, the easy way.

HE'S THE FLYING CHAMP

Hawk

It has been said that learning to fly is like joining a nudist colony . . . you'll never forget that first take-off! And learning that one of the most maligned birds on earth mates for life, is a considerate parent, kills only for food and not for sport, makes an obedient and loving pet, and saves farmers untold dollars in rodent control, is usually as surprising to most folks as finding out that you can't bounce a meatball.

The bird under scrutiny here is a hawk, not just one, but the hawks in general. The doves will have to wait before they get equal time. Most of us usually classify hawks into just two groups-----the big and the little, that kill chickens, drive the farmers to distraction, and are bloodthirsty. The truth of the matter is that there are thirty-two species of hawks found in North America and that very few of them eat chickens or game birds. Ah, you ask, how the heck do they know? Well sir, the U.S. Department of Agriculture analyzed the stomachs of almost 2,700 hawks and found that mostly they dined on rodents, destructive birds, and pesky insects, had no ulcers, and rarely took baking soda at bedtime.

The eye of the eagle has nothing on the hawk. Whether the hawk is as small as a swallow or large enough to clobber an antelope, his eyes are sharp enough to spot a birdwatcher a mile away. His eyeballs are sometimes as large as a human's with a retina twice the thickness of man's. In addition, the lens changes shape in a twinkling so that the eye actually works like a quick focusing telescope varying from farsightedness, to nearsightedness quicker than you can say "Murine."

As if that isn't enough to drive an oculist up the wall, the hawk has a great little device to cut down the glare of bright daylight. His eyes secrete drops of yellow oil that coat the eyeball just like dropping a filter on the lens or the shades on the orbs. And while his brain isn't among the largest (after all, he has a bird-brain), he's still smart enough to insulate his nest with fresh sticks and stuff when he heads south for the winter, so that the nest will withstand the fury of winter and be intact when he gets back. He's also savvy enough to fly with a fish in his claws, holding the fish's head into the wind to cut downair resistance.

The peregrine falcon is the champion flyer of the bird world, wheeling and whirring and diving at speeds of 250 miles an hour, and maneuvering in a manner that would make an aerobatic pilot turn a bright shade of chartreuse with envy. During the mating season hawks have even been seen wildly diving, somersaulting at the bottom of the dive, and somersaulting again at the top of the pullout, and then throwing in a few barrelrolls to really "turn on" their screeching mates! Now that's flying! And no worry about hijacking either.

Hawks are senselessly slaughtered every year. The protection of these precious birds is gaining, I'm happy to report, but it'll take more than just "laws." Just as birds flock together, humans will have to band together and help. The wild beauty of a serenely soaring or daredevil diving hawk is something to see, to treasure. Let's keep it that way.

Blue Heron

A Russian scientist named Pavlov, studying digestion, once trained his dog to salivate only when a bell was rung. Another scientist recently conditioned his dog to eat only when he heard chimes, and then didn't feed his dog for ten days. When the doorbell rang, it was goodbye Avon lady! The big blue heron needs neither bells nor chimes, he just eats whenever he can spear frogs or small fish with his needle-nosed bill. A neat trick when you consider that the heron uses his head like a spear with eyes.

There are sixty kinds of herons and bitterns in the same family, all of them just mediocre flyers but great waders, all having long skinny legs, long skinny toes, and long skinny necks, and most of them living in marshes and swamps where the food is plentiful and the feet stay wet. Perfect spot to open a shoestore that specializes in galoshes.

The great blue heron is the big boy of American herons with a tip to tip wingspread of close to six feet, which is two feet longer than his height, or four feet, which not too many folks care about because they confuse herons with cranes anyhow. However, if you'd like to straighten out the visual difference, next time you see a big bird fly and swear that it's a heron, merely check the neck. If he flies with the neck outstretched, he's a crane, if the neck is tucked back on his shoulders, S-shaped, he's a heron. And if he's holding a cocktail glass in his claw, he's the editor and is classified as the "double-ruffed martini-lifter or red-eyed lush." A most common species hereabouts.

The great blue heron is just barely blue, more of a washed out gray with bluish overtones. He appears dark blue at a distance, and even a little brown sometimes when he flies slowly but steadily. Oftimes several nests will be in a single tree, and as often as possible those trees will be on islands as far from the guns of hunters as they can possibly get. Which seems to make sense. Mama Blue Heron will lay three to four light blue eggs at one sitting, or rather setting, and then keep the helpless little ones in the nest until they're able to fly, feeding them by urping up a partly digested frog, fish, or water snake, and poking it down into their yawning little gullets. Mothers with feeding problems, take note.

Big Blue is a somewhat timid bird, but if ever cornered, he'll use his six-inch bill much the same as a bayonet, striking with incredible swiftness, and usually at the eyes of the enemy. And he has a peculiar habit of standing on one leg when he sleeps. No one really knows why, but if he's happy with less "understanding" who are we to educate him?

YOU'LL NEVER SADDLE THIS RIVER HORSE

Hippopotamus

The Greeks had a word for it, and *Hippo-potamus* is the word. Translated it means "river horse," a most appropriate description. His size is probably the most striking thing you'll notice about a hippo, because he can weigh up to 8,000 pounds, stand about 4-1/2 feet at the shoulder, and get to be about 17 feet long—add another foot for his dinky tail. His large, round body is set on stumpy legs, so short that you marvel at how this big blob of blubber can walk without scraping a couple of layers of hide from the bottom of the more than ample belly. His head alone can weigh as much as 2,000 pounds. Can you imagine what it would be like to have a headache in a one ton head? You'd have to take an eight pound aspirin.

The hippo at one time lived in Europe, ranging up into the Thames valley, which would, of course, make punting on the Thames a most thrilling experience, because the hippo has been known to literally chew a boat to pieces if it irritated him in passing. And that goes for the occupants as well. Anyhow, the portly creature is now almost exclusively north of Zululand in Africa, living cheek to jowl with the deadly crocodile . . . and the fearsome reptiles don't mess around with a hopped-up Hippo, for the powerful teeth of a hippo can rip through the armorplated hide of the largest crocodile in one large bite.

He's not an especially good swimmer, neither fast nor adept, but he can sure float like a champion. What he can do best is walk along the bottom of the lake or river in shallow water, rooting up water plants with his tusks. And he's strong enough to buck a rapid current and sort of dog paddle his way upstream. Not only can he float like a four ton bubble, but he can also sink like a streamlined rock and run along the bottom at about eight miles an hour. The average time this dark brown living submarine stays under water is about two minutes at a time, but he has been known to take the deep six for thirty minutes at a time, and that's enough to give you water on the knee.

From time to time a circus will advertise a hippo in their side show that actually "sweats blood," and it certainly looks like he does, as a thick, oily, red secretion oozes out onto the surface of the skin. Oil it is, but blood it is not. The hippo has special glands, you see, that compensate for the time he's out of the water, when his skin dries out too much, by secreting this thick, oily substance to lubricate his skin; and some experts even think it also works to keep his skin pliable when he's in the water too much. Max Factor, Helena Rubenstein, and the Avon lady, please pay attention.

The only mammal with a mouth larger than the hippo is the whale, and old big mouth hippo seems to like to open his just for fun or maybe to just show off his teeth, which are formidable, to say the least. Some of his teeth are as much as twenty-four inches long, about half of this length below the gum line. One tooth alone can weigh up to seven pounds. Look, Ma, no cavities! The teeth are ideally suited for cutting water plants, long grasses, or tall reeds, on which the hippo feeds. The tusks are worth a great deal as a source of ivory, although they're much more brittle than an elephant's tusks.

He's related to the pig and certainly eats like one, and I'm sure he never heard of Metrecal. The hippo is considered quite a delightful food by many tribesmen in Africa, one animal yielding as much as 200 pounds of fat, and, as we all know, hippo fat makes an excellent soup----I'll bet. The natives say, though, that the fat rendered down to lard never goes rancid, and they love it. The meat itself is stringy and tastes like a hunk of horse well basted in 3-in-1 Oil. Pass the breaded hippo hocks, please.

A BILL WITHOUT CREDIT

CHAS. HERZOG III

Hornbill

Why did the chicken cross the road? Why, to get away from Colonel Sanders, of course. And why is the hot dog the noblest of all dogs? Because it feeds the hand that bites it! Now, why do the hornbills of Asia and Africa hatch their eggs in prison? Well, not actually in prison, but the hornbills do indeed have the most remarkable nesting habits of any found among birds.

When a boy hornbill and a girl hornbill have an urge to merge and build a nest, they go apartment hunting, looking for a tree with a hollow large enough to house the female. She, big billed and sexy, builds a nest inside the hollow, while the male gathers mud, dung, and debris. He swallows these materials, and later urps them up as small, sticky pellets which he passes on to his mate in the hollow of the tree. Talk about bad breath, well sir!

Anyhow, this adobe-like material is taken by the female who immediately starts sealing herself into her chamber, à la *The Cask of Amontillado,* leaving only a slit-like window just big enough for papa's bill to poke inside. And that's being plastered the hard way. For the next six to eight weeks the male is both attentive and anxious and runs himself ragged feeding his imprisoned wife, who meanwhile has laid a few white eggs. When the female and the young finally come out of the cozy prison, the male is skinny and bedraggled, while mama is resplendent in a brand new feather outfit, having molted completely while mothering and incubating. Maybe that's the way to get a new Easter outfit, Mother, give birth.

The hornbill is a fairly large bird, with the most prominent feature being, as you might have guessed by now, the bill. It's so large that he looks like he's out of balance, like he ought to fall flat on his face. And, as if he needs it, on top of this big beak, he has a pretty good sized, brightly colored growth called a *casque.* You might think that all this equipment would be heavy and really weigh him down, and you might start shouting, "He'll never fly, he'll never get off the ground," but the beak and the casque are made of extra-light, thin-walled hollow cells and weigh hardly anything at all.

Hornbills have short legs and weak feet, and don't spend too much time walking around, but they do hop from bough to bough on the tops of fruit trees eating most of the day, and in the evening they sluggishly and slowly fly to the ground to bathe and feed some more, all the while hopping around like snockered seagulls with sore feet. There are forty-six species of hornbills and most are black and white and occasionally chestnut or gray colored. It is said that when they get a sinus attack and a cold and a stuffed-up beak----they really pay through the nose!

CHAS. HERZOG III

Hummingbird

"Why do hummingbirds hum?"
"Because they don't know the words!"

Very funny, but not very accurate. Actually, hummingbirds don't hum, but they do beat their wings in oval circles at close to seventy-five wingbeats a second, so fast that to the human eye only a blur is visible and the whirring sound the wings make give the bird its name. It's a hummer, all right, especially when hovering and feeding on a nectar-laden flower.

Some naturalists consider hummingbirds the most beautiful birds in the world, and certainly one of the most wondrous. On short dashes they're probably the swiftest of all birds, moving so quickly, darting so speedily, that they almost look as though they were shot from Robin Hood's bow. Of all the 8,600 kinds of birds, only these little iridescent gems are able to truly fly backwards. They use their strong little wings much the same as today's modern helicopters. And the wings are indeed strong, necessarily so, because these superb little flyers spend most of their active hours in the air, eating on the wing, so to speak, with the help of a pretty specialized kind of bill.

Sometimes the bill of the hummingbird will get as long as five inches with a slight downward curve and a needle-like point, although some of the bills on some of the birds are nearly straight. And to fill the bill, a specialized kind of tongue, too. A tongue that's tubular and long enough to reach deep into the inner recesses of certain flowers, sucking up not only nectar, but tiny insects and spiders as well. Since he flits from flower to flower, he also plays the part of an insect, pollinating as he pops from bloom to bloom like a perkie pixie on a pogo stick.

Hummingbirds are primarily active during the day, and most of them are found along the edges of forests where flowers bloom in the spring tra-la. And where there are many flowers, there are many little feathered beauties, which give the impression that they like to flock together and enjoy group living. That isn't exactly true—they're just there because that's where the lunchroom is. And if you'd like to approximate the sound that a hummingbird makes, just unscrew a rusty cap from an old pickle jar. They sing with feeble cheeps or squeaks, like hungover weathermen.

Hummingbirds are either fearless or just birdbrained when it comes to fearing man, because they readily flit about in his presence, and they seem to be just as courageous when it comes to other animals that come close to their nests. Their nests are about the size of a two-bit piece, and usually found around twenty feet off the ground, astraddle a tree limb. The nest is usually made of plant cotton, decorated with lichens, and reinforced with spider webs, just right to hold the two tiny white eggs, which are about the size of two emaciated sweet peas.

There are 319 kinds of hummingbirds, 18 varieties in the United States, and only one, the ruby-throated hummingbird, lives east of the Mississippi. Maybe he knows something. Anyhow, old Ruby Throat can fly at speeds of up to fifty-five miles an hour, which is freeway speed. His wife and children don't share his coloration. They're white and green, and can't sing either, but they stick together nonetheless, because to a hummingbird-----there's no place like HUM!

TALK ABOUT AN EASY RIDER!

Forester Kangaroo

Once upon a time, it is said, a mama kangaroo scolded her youngster . . . "How many times have I told you not to eat crackers in bed!" But the truth of the matter is that kangaroos don't eat crackers or meat or much else except vegetation. And baby kangaroos don't feed on anything but mother's milk for at least the first six months of their life. The first six months are spent in the pocket or pouch found on the undersurface of mama's body.

It's hard to believe that an animal that grows as large as 6 feet tall and can weigh up to 200 pounds is no larger than an inch long and about 1/4 inch in diameter at birth, but that's about the size of it. And even stranger than that truth is the fact that it's born and then makes its way all by itself, with unerring instinct, through the hair to the pouch, where it attaches itself so firmly to one of the milk taps that it's almost impossible to dislodge, which gives rise to the false belief that a kangaroo is not born like other mammals, but simply grows from the belly of its mother.

Kangaroos are found mainly in Australia, as are most of the marsupials of the world. Some of the islands of the South Pacific, like Tasmania and New Guinea, and some sections of South and Central America have a few marsupials still around, but they're definitely in the minority. Just what does "marsupial" mean anyhow? Well sir, it's from the Latin word that means "pouch", and of course, only the female has it. Although, one wag has it, that the male also has a pouch, but just a small one—just large enough to carry his wallet in. Not so.

The great kangaroo, or Forester, is the largest of all the kangaroos, and to most of us, the most familiar type. He has long hind legs and big feet for hopping and leaping. His tail is long and mighty powerful, used mostly for balance and propping himself when at rest, and not so much as an aid in jumping, though jump he can. When in a hurry he can cover as much as twenty feet in a single bound, and there's a story about a kangaroo, being chased by dogs, that soared over a mass of dead timber ten and a half feet high—the length of the leap was twenty-seven feet! Maybe we ought to forget putting a tiger in our tank, and slip a kangaroo in—for short hops!

Kangaroos are relatively gentle in nature, timid and harmless—unless they're cornered and pushed into defending themselves, and then they can become as dangerous as playing touch tag with a snorting rhino. A large male can more than hold his own if backed against a tree or wall, with reports of whole packs of dogs being held at bay, with the pooch that got too courageous being torn to shreds by the powerful clawed hind feet. Not the ideal kind of animal to be taught to box, yet there are many stories of boxing kangaroos, and most of them are true.

Kangaroos in the wild sometimes amuse themselves by sparring with each other, and with very little training in captivity they can be taught to box "on cue." What happens if the big fellow gets mad, though, and decides to fight dirty? And can he take a punch in the paunch? Who knows and who cares? Maybe when the champ runs out of challengers he might consider Kanvasback Kangaroo not much at jabbing, but a terror at in-fighting.

A herd of kangaroos is called a *mob,* and in the days of long ago a mob of 1,000 head wasn't too unusual. Today it's doubtful that a mob of 100 could be found. A young kangaroo is called a "joey," which is much better than being called a "marvin." And wouldn't it be great if they could cross a kangaroo with a horse? Then the cowboys could ride inside when it rained!

Kinkajou

It looks like a cat, acts like a monkey, and lives like an old fashioned playboy—sleeping all day, staying up all night, and loving his honey . . . the kind of honey that comes in a hive, that is.

Of course, that description could fit many other animals, but the one we're talking about is the kute, kantankerous, kanny, and kunning kinkajou, a long tongued, short furred, long tailed, short legged relative of the raccoon. The kinkajou can be found in the tropics from southern Mexico to southern Brazil, and with the kind of winters we have up north, maybe he's smarter than we think.

The kinkajou is not only quicker than a sore-eyed wink, but he has a tail that's stronger than garlic in a moustache, and this wondrous tail is probably his most outstanding feature. With this long, strong tail he can not only reach out and grasp food he couldn't reach with his hands, but the strength of this grasping "fifth hand" is incredible. It's been said that when he's got this steel cable tail wrapped around a branch, and at the same time is holding on to the tree with all four feet, nothing short of a full-fledged tornado or a sudden heart attack, can dislodge it-----almost as hard to remove as a grease spot on a silk tie.

In Mexico they call it the *mico leon* which means "monkey-lion", because it's said that they like to mangle monkeys—but that's not true at all. It's also said that they become lovable pets when tamed—but that's because not many people who write about kinkajous have ever owned one. The truth of the matter is that they seem to be emotionally unstable and if things don't go their way, they go into a titanic tizzy, and woe to the owner of this "lovable pet" if he doesn't get him back in the cage quickly, which could be as difficult as putting an oyster in a piggy bank.

They'll eat most anything, but they seem to like fruit best—especially wild figs, using their educated tongues to dig out the pulpy meat. They'll also eat insects, fish, reptiles, and birds, and certainly don't turn their noses up at mushrooms. Might make a good toadstool tester. Sometimes the kinkajou is called the "honey bear" because one of his favorite delicacies is honey. He's perfectly adapted for tearing open a hive or a honey tree with his powerful forearms and slurping up the nectar with his extremely long tongue, which comes in mighty handy at Christmas time for licking stamps. The bees buzzing and bombing, singing and stinging don't seem to bother him at all.

Maybe it's the sugar in alcohol, or maybe they're just natural born lushes, but kinkajous have an unquenchable thirst when it comes to booze. They just don't seem to get enough alcohol if given access to it. And brand name doesn't make any difference—anything from Vitalis to Royal Crown to just plain "home squeezings." And once they're loaded, look out! They become violent and vicious, which isn't such a far cry from some two-legged animals called *homo sapiens.*

These little tree climbers, lithe and lively, get from place to place by swinging through the trees monkey-fashion, rarely getting to the ground, resting now and then by just hanging by the tail. The tail is about twenty-two inches long, which is a trifle longer than its head and body together. The fur is thick, soft as owl feathers, and generally honey yellow in color, and while they're fun to look at in a zoo, they rarely move during the day. And so most zoos fool them into thinking it's night time by use of special "infrared lights," thereby reversing their life cycle. In other words they're on NST-----Nightlight Savings Time.

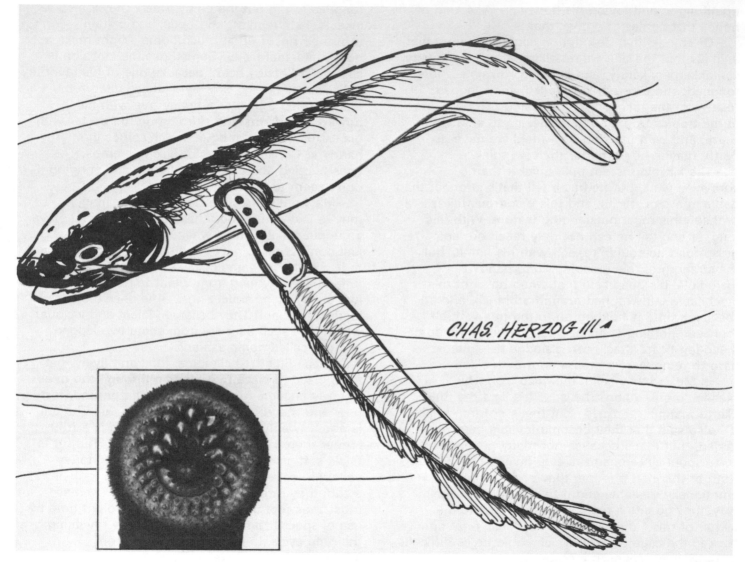

Sea Lamprey

Show me a fish that can't close its mouth, can climb up cliffs, has only one nostril, no scales, and is slimier than oil on an oyster, and I'll show you one of the most repulsive creatures that ever swam in our seas.

It's the sea lamprey we're feeling a little bilious about here. A fish that not only looks like a vaselined eel, but lives the kind of life that would make a scavenging buzzard look like a vegetarian by comparison. Even a hyena wouldn't laugh. And it seems almost incredible that during the Middle Ages lampreys were considered a delicacy by the nobility, with King Henry the First of England throwing off this mortal coil as a result of eating too many. There's just no accounting for taste.

There are about twenty-five different kinds of lampreys found in both fresh and salt water, and all of them are listed among the most primitive of animals with vertebrae. They all have mouths like the Detroit-Windsor tunnel with teeth. Instead of jaws, the mouth is surrounded by a band of cartilage lined with hundreds of sharp teeth. It never closes! They have punch-press tongues, also studded with teeth, that they use to rasp their way onto and into their victim's bodies so that their suction-like mouths can firmly attach themselves and suck the very life from other fishes. There are even records of lampreys attaching themselves to human swimmers, or to speedboats passing by at fifteen miles an hour. Not very bright parasites, but they've got a lot of pull, or rather, suction.

Saltwater lampreys come into fresh water to breed, and as they go upstream sometimes find their way blocked by a waterfall. It only slows them up a little. They just use their suckerlike mouths to attach themselves to rocks, hold against the current, and then gradually work themselves forward, swim a little, attach to a rock a little, and then swim a little more. They can also do this up the face of cliffs over which the water is rushing, and man, that's what I call stick-to-it-iveness.

The sea lamprey only has one nostril: it sits between two pretty good-sized eyes, and behind each eye is a series of holes which lead right into the gills, so that he can breathe without letting his "plumber's friend" mouth come away from the host fish. It just doesn't make sense when you're having dinner on a friend, to let him swim away.

The body of this eel-like vacuum sweeper sometimes gets up to three feet long. Lampreys have no scales, and the skin varies from whitish on the belly to grayish blue on the back, and mottled as they get older. The skin secretes so much slime that it's almost impossible to hold one in your hand, as if you'd want to.

Sea lampreys can live in fresh water, as most folks in the Michigan area know. Several years ago this watery vampire made its way through the St. Lawrence Seaway into the Great Lakes and became a serious pest as it attacked the lake trout. If only the lamprey could suck up mercury too! As far as I'm concerned, this left-over from a science fiction movie could give charisma lessons to the Beast From 20,000 Fathoms.

THE TRAVELING LEMMING

Lemming

Why does a man stand with his back to the fire? Hard to say, but one explanation I read not too long ago blames it on the great flood of Biblical times, when Noah's ark sprang a leak and old man Noah sent a dog to plug the hole. All he did was sniff at it. Noah then sent a woman, but all she did was step on it. Poor Noah then sent a man, and using his head, he sat on it, stopping the leak. Since then, all dogs have cold noses, all women have cold feet-----and all men stand with their backs to fires. Now, if it were only as easy to answer the question "why do lemmings, thousands upon thousands strong, migrate?" Why do they, every four years, seem to commit mass suicide by drowning?

Actually, these chubby little six-inch rodents don't deliberately commit suicide, they're just looking for food and living space, and it just happens that the natural migration path along river valleys and lake systems leads to the sea. The poor little lemmings usually start their headlong, unstoppable dash in the late winter or early spring, scurrying around trees, over stones, through bushes, frantically barking in shrill little piping voices. Some of them die of exhaustion, some try swimming a lake and become meals for the voracious pike, some of them reach the sea and just continue swimming until they too become exhausted and drown. Even the caribou jump on the free lunch wagon, crushing the little creatures in their teeth and swallowing them whole, while gulls, hawks, cats, foxes, bears and owls all get their share without having to hunt or chase. If I were a lemming, I think I'd hibernate every fourth year and also take out a lot of insurance.

The matter of the mass migration isn't fully understood, though. Sheer overcrowding and lack of food is probably the main reason. Stress symptoms have been observed in lemmings, the only known example of this human complaint in wild animals. The Eskimos and the peasants of northern Europe explain the lemmings' sudden appearance every four years quite simply. They say that the animals spiral down from the sky in a snowstorm. Another theory is that the Scandinavian lemmings reach their peak in population every fourth year and are driven by instinct to search for their ancient home, which some say, is on the submerged land of Atlantis! Maybe it's a combination of all explanations plus sunspots and atomic explosions. Who knows?

We do know, however, that the lemming has long soft fur, a short, one inch tail, and hair on the bottom of his feet to protect them from snow and ice. He's usually buff colored, with black markings on his head and shoulders, plus bright little eyes and sharp little teeth. His nest is built on the surface of the ground and covered with moss and vegetation and in the winter when the nest is covered by a nice thick blanket of snow, he is relatively safe from birds, beasts and winter's cruel icy winds. He easily finds food under the snow, nibbling on the dried grasses and stuff, and has plenty of time to raise a nice litter of six to fill the nest. Now, if he could only stifle that inherited urge to travel.

A CRAFTY CAT

CHAS. HERZOG III

Leopard

Once upon a time an enterprising bachelor went to a computer dating service and listed his specific requirements for a mate. He wanted someone on the small side, who liked water sports, was friendly, liked formal dress, and didn't talk too much----he got a penguin! It's a good thing he didn't specify someone who is graceful, weighs about a 100 pounds, likes fur coats, is quick to learn, and loves to go out at night to eat----he might have gotten a leopard!

The folks who live in Africa say they'd rather have a showdown with a lion than a leopard, because the leopard is much more savage and much cleverer than either the lion or the tiger. Not only does he move with the speed of spotted lightning, he's also a clever tracker, using his super-cat intelligence to ambush a careless dinner. If that doesn't work, he'll use a ruse to snare an unwary deer. For instance, the wily leopard has been seen rolling on the ground like a great big "putty-tat," just being coy and playful, while a nearby deer, with its curiosity piqued, moves in for a closer look. The closer he gets, the more the big cat plays, until the distance is narrowed, the curiosity dulled, the trap triggered, and the poor deer a victim.

Not only does this fierce and somewhat treacherous cat like deer, but he loves antelope, monkeys, cattle, and sheep, to say nothing of dog meat. It's this love of dog meat that makes him such a threat to humans, because that's what brings him into the compound. Under ordinary conditions a leopard won't attack a man, but most men will try to protect their cattle, sheep, or dogs, and that's when the fierce feline gets the reputation of being a man killer----sometimes.

Leopards are found in Burma, the Malay Peninsula, Africa, India, Ceylon, and even north up into parts of Siberia, and they come in various sizes, from five feet long to nine feet long, including the long and switching tail. The average weight is about 100 pounds, and they rarely live beyond 20 years. Way back, when the Big Dipper was just a drinking cup, and Howard Johnson only had one flavor, folks used to think that the leopard and the panther were two different animals. Not so, not so. The only difference was size, and sometimes color. Just variations on a theme, as it were.

The typical leopard has large and small black spots scattered over a buff-colored fur, in a rosette or circle, four or five spots to the circle. But there are slight differences, depending on the climate and the country. Hot country, short hair, cooler climes, longer fur, with the most striking difference being the black panther, which is still the fierce, savage, deceitful, beautiful leopard, whose spots are still there, you just can't see them too easily. Under the right light, you can just see the markings, as though he still needed a spot remover to remove the spots left by a spot remover!

CHAS. HERZOG III

Lion

Is the lion really the king of beasts? Is he aggressive, vicious, crafty, sly, and sometimes valorous? Maybe he's like the lion in the Land of Oz, cowardly, or lazy and not too bright. Well, whatever he is, he's an animal that commands respect.

This overgrown cat reaches a length of eight feet, and can weigh around 600 pounds. Couple this size with powerful muscles, litheness, and an empty belly, add a full set of sabre-like teeth and claws, and you have an incredibly efficient and fearsome killing machine. Not the kind of animal you'd ask "What's new pussycat?"

Lions once covered Africa from Gibraltar to the Cape, and extended from Turkey to India and Arabia. They even wandered as far north as Italy, getting into a form of show business playing the Coliseum with frightening regularity. However, today the only place you find our regal friends is southern Africa and in zoos all over the world. They breed so well in captivity that they're virtually without value in the haggling places of the zoo market. With many animals the problem is getting them, with the lion the problem is getting rid of them. Maybe, if we taught them to block and tackle we could sell them to a football team in Detroit. The team has the name and it might improve their game . . .

It may come as a small surprise, but it's the female lion who brings home the bacon. She actually does the stalking and the killing. About the only thing lordly Leo does is stand around looking regal and fierce, maybe roaring now and then to drive the prey toward mama's jaws and claws. After the kill, he dashes in, takes the lion's share, eats his fill, belches loudly, and leaves the rest of the kill for the females and the cubs, while he goes back to pose for more pictures on the MGM stage.

In the wild the lion's favorite dish is the succulent zebra—at least during his youth. When he starts thinking of the jungle rocking chair, when his teeth, like bowlegs, become few and far between, when his legs lose their spring, then he'll eat whatever is available—small mice, an occasional bird, slugs, scorpions, and any other animal he's capable of catching. Despite the popular belief that these older lions sometimes turn man-eaters, it's the youngsters who really give the trouble. For some not readily explainable reason, some young lions turn into juvenile delinquents and hunt and devour man. Then, as quick as they start, they stop. The lion who continues to be a man-eater throughout his life is virtually unknown.

They're pretty fair tree climbers and it's not unusual to see them sleeping off a meal in the crotch of a tree high off the ground, their tails flicking spasmodically. And the tale of the tail of a lion is another argument no one has really ever settled. The tip of the tail is tufted with dark brown or black hairs, and it is said that hidden completely in this tuft is a "spur" or "claw" that the lion uses to whip himself into a fury before attacking . . . Only the lion knows for sure, and he's not talking, roaring a little, maybe, but not talking.

And something that all cat lovers know is that a cat's tongue is rougher than a stucco soup spoon, only in the lion it's even more so. He can literally lick the flesh from a bone without the use of his teeth----tongue alone. As a result some of the food particles remain on the rasp-like tongue, decay through the day, and give the lion one of the greatest cases of halitosis in the animal world, breath strong enough to color Easter eggs. However, there're not many animals in the animal kingdom who would dare to go up to the lion and say, "I really don't like to say this, boss, but you've got bad breath." Wouldn't that make a terrible television commercial?

THE LLAMA'S SPITTIN' IMAGE

Llama

It has been said that you cannot expectorate at will and still expect to rate the admiration of your friends. And you can't be fooling around with a llama and not expect to be spat upon, because that's one of its favorite methods of showing displeasure. Llamas can pucker up and splatter the object of their displeasure with amazing accuracy, a disgusting mess of half-digested grass that's blasted through the mouth and nose. Even the baby llamas are spitting images of their parents . . .

The camel, the llama, the alpaca, guanaco, and vicuna are all related quite closely. While the camel, the animal that supposedly looks like it was put together by a committee, lives mostly on the desert, the others all live on mountain slopes or lush grassy plains. The alpaca and the llama have been domesticated for over 3,000 years, and their cousins, the guanaco and the vicuna, can still be found in the wilds of South America, although, they too have been domesticated.

The llama is not only the strongest, but the largest of all the South American species, over four feet tall at the shoulder and as sure-footed as the legendary mountain goat. Llamas are great beasts of burden and easily tote between 150 and 200 pounds for great distances over impossible, impassable terrain. And talk about independence----well sir, if the llama is ever overloaded, he doesn't file a grievance report, he doesn't lash out angrily, he doesn't bray, bellow, or bellyache—he just sits down on the job.

Once he's down, no amount of cudgeling or cajoling will get him up until the overload is removed. And if you push him too far, as we said before, he'll spit in your eye. Only the male of the specie is put to work as a pack animal, the females are used exclusively for breeding purposes. Women's Lib, where are you?

The Spaniards, when they first came to the New World in the sixteenth century, called these handy, dandy animals "Peruvian sheep." To the ancient Inca these wondrous beasts were life itself, much the same as the buffalo was to the American Indian. The meat was mighty good to eat, the wool was light, warm and soft and ideal for clothing and blankets. The hide made fine sandals, the fat turned into candles that were just right for reading in bed, ropes were made from some of the hair, and even the body waste was used for fuel, not too aromatic, but inexpensive and readily available—everywhere.

And just to show you how valuable these animals were to the Incas, how much they appreciated them, they sacrificed them at religious festivals. Some honor! Each god had a different color llama as his very own. The biggest god got a brown llama, the sun god got a white one, and the ones that were mixed in color, brown, black, and white, reminded the Incas of clouds and so they were sacrificed to the god of thunder. But, surprisingly enough, the poor Incas went the way of all .150 hitters, and the llamas survived the test of time.

LOUIE THE LUNGFISH

African Lungfish

It's been said that you can be sure you're ready for a vacation when someone has to explain the plot of the "Beverly Hillbillies" to you; when you take your sox off over your head—and make it; or when you suddenly can't stand the noise of the neighbor's ironing. That may be true for you, but for the African lungfish it's a much easier process. He begins to suspect that he'll be "out of it" for awhile when the stream, lake, river, or swamp he's living in begins to dry up and go away.

When the dry season or long drought sets in, this strange fish sinks slowly into the mud and gets ready for his long withdrawal by folding his tail over his head in sort of a U-shaped position, head and tail near the top of the U. Then through a process known only to the clever lungfish, he covers himself with a thin coat of fishy slime to keep his body from drying out completely as the mud around him hardens into a cement-like condition, and there he stays, as quiet as a New York taxi driver saying "thank you." He stays there until the rains come and soften the mud again, and revive old Louie the Lungfish. And you thought you were a hardy sleeper!

This poor fish has the record for living longer without food and water than any other backboned animal in the world. We know of some of these strange creatures that have been kept in their state of suspended animation for more than four years! Of course, once they wake up and start living more like a fish than a fossil, they start to eat like Rip Van Winkle on the morning after, gobbling up other fishes, snails, clams, anything they can wrap their lips around.

The secret of this "estivation," or long rest, is the ability to slow up his body functions to a point where they're almost as inactive as a stopped watch. He's an air breather, and so, even when he's encased in the brick of mud, there's always a little opening or two for the air to sneak through. And when he's swimming like any other fish, he still has to scurry up to the surface every twenty minutes or so, and gulp a little of the unpolluted African ozone. If he doesn't surface now and then, quite simply, he drowns. He's certainly one of nature's most peculiar piscatorial products.

The lungfish's body is long with long fins that come together giving him a pretty sharp pointed tail; his scales are somewhat on the teeny-weeny side and completely embedded in the skin; while his color varies from brown to black to tan or a combination of all three. There are three kinds of these wacky wonders swimming around in the fresh waters of Africa, ranging in size from three feet long to six feet long, and from what we hear, they're mighty good eating. Can't you just hear someone in a restaurant asking if the fish is fresh today, and hearing, "Yessir—we just chopped him out of a cement fishbowl this morning!"

CHAS. HERZOG III

Canadian Lynx

You don't always find gloves in a glove compartment, pants in a pantry, or horse in horseradish, and you don't always find the Canadian lynx in Canada. Sometimes this wild and wily animal is spotted in Colorado, Oregon, or even northern New York, but mostly he lives in the north country of Canada where the evergreens, the fallen timber, and the rough landscape make it a haven for a lynx and a hard way to go for a man.

The solemn looking lynx with the "hip" side whiskers has silky soft fur, long and lovely, not only warm but nice to look at, and it's no wonder he'd like to wear it himself, but the mighty Nimrod, the happy hunter, thinks it looks better on the chick of his choice, and as a result the unlucky lynx is too often separated from his grayish-brown, spotted in black, hide. And you thought that the fox was the lynx's worst enemy!

The bobcat, the wild cat, and the bay lynx are all related to the Canadian lynx; they're just not as large, that's all, and they all have tails that are shorter than a week when you're on vacation, hence the name *bobcat*. The hind legs of the Canadian cat are exceptionally long, and you get the impression that he's running downhill all the time; while his feet are not really in proportion with his three foot long body. They're especially large, broad, and well padded, so that he can make good time as he gallops awkwardly across the snow in pursuit of his favorite tidbit, the snowshoe rabbit.

The face of the lynx is most interesting. A cynical, crafty, curious, and cunning cat-face, surrounded by pointed ears, and furry ruffs. The black edging around the ruff and ears gives him a sort of kingly but kooky look. Unlike most cats he likes water, and seems to enjoy a dip now and then, and those who know, say he dog-paddles as well as any poodle can paddle. Would you say he's a cat who's gone to the dogs?

The lovely lynx hunts mostly at night with eyes that are sharper than a serpent's tooth. When snowshoe rabbits are scarcer than acorns in the petrified forest, he'll settle for an unwary beaver or two. Sometimes he'll sneak up on a small deer, when the soft-eyed creature is lying down, and spring like a speeding arrow straight to the poor deer's throat, where he clamps his sharp teeth and hangs on till death do them part. Survival of the fittest, fattest, and fastest, as it were.

About four little kittens are the average litter for Mama Lynx who cares for her little furballs quite carefully, nursing them for two months or so, until they're old enough to go hunting with mama and papa. After about a year of this listening to their elders, they attain their maturity, break all the family ties, and tell their parents to hit the road. Then they find a mate, join a protest movement, make their own enemies, think they know it all, answer the call of the Wild, and start all over again just so there'll never be any missing lynx in the chain of nature. It's like threading beads on a string with no knot on the end.

MANDRILL THE MONSTER
WON'T EAT PEOPLE

Mandrill

If you were casting a horror picture like *The Squash That Ate the World and Found Indigestion,* and needed a monster with a fearsome face to play the lead, whom or what would you consider? Suppose the author described the monster as having eyes like a pig, a muzzle like a dog with blue, red, scarlet, white, black, and yellow markings on his face. No, the tax collector doesn't get the part, but a mandrill would.

The wild and weird-looking mandrills are strong, savage, and sturdy baboons that prowl the forest in groups of fifty or so, the young screaming, the others rooting, grunting, and screeching as they move from place to place. They don't like people, but they love to eat other things, like fruit, eggs, insects, reptiles, amphibians, roots, and even a mammal or two if it's not too much trouble. They'll eat anything they can get in their mouths.

And you'll have to admit that this fierce animal is colorful, as colorful as a revolving rainbow in fact, because he's many-hued no matter which way he turns. Not only do the scarlet furrows on his face slash across the vivid blue swellings along the sides of his nose, but the tip of his nose is bright red, he has yellow-white patches above each ear that extend around his neck, a black dot in the middle of his forehead and a yellow beard, like a clown with inborn makeup! And at the other end there are great patches of red, as though he's got a built-in cushion for comfortable sitting. Actually, the red behind is a sex symbol and the color changes in intensity at different times from violent violet to crazy crimson. He's the kind of beast that only a mother could love, and then only if she were nearsighted.

Mandrills walk on all fours, and a troop of these ugly baboons, some as large as three feet long, baring their inch long fangs, their black hair bristling, is more exciting than seeing a karate expert beaten up by an interior decorator. Mandrills spend most of their lives on the ground, with an occasional climb into a tree to relieve the monotony, and while they don't really have one particular home, they do have a territory or turf that they control, and it would be nonhabit forming for another troop or company to muscle in. The protection racket won't work either.

This wild, wise, and weird monkey, this strong, savage, sly creature, has an ugly disposition when molested, and while lions or leopards may attack a youngster or weaker female, a group of males would easily tear such a predator to shreds with their powerful jaws and slashing teeth. And if you think that would be something to watch, you ought to see an agressive male fight for one of the females in his harem! The battle may start between two males, but in nothing flat the entire troop is involved in biting, scratching, clawing, screaming, ripping, and tearing, like a TV studio two minutes before airtime. The fight doesn't last long, and the victor usually gets what's left of the female, which is just about a claw, a bone, and a hank of hair. Statistics show, that among the mandrills, deaths are high, divorces low.

DOES A MANTIS PRAY OR PREY?

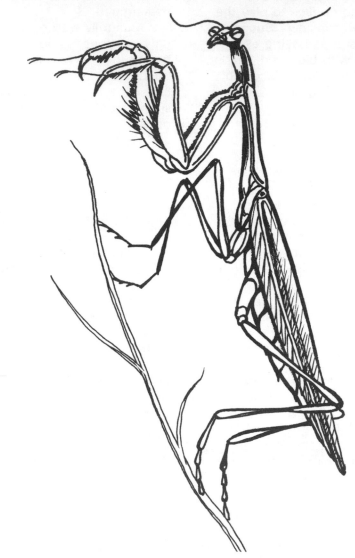

Preying Mantis

How do you keep germs from spreading? Get 'em a girdle! How do you get help for gardeners whose plants are being eaten up by insects? Simple----just import an insect that eats insects that eat garden plants! And that's precisely how the preying mantis got into the United States. He was brought over from China about seventy years ago because the bigdomes of the agriculture world felt he would be helpful and eat only the bad bugs, but the truth of the matter is, that he eats as many good guys as bad guys. But here he is and here he'll stay.

If you should get one of these sneaky, posturing bugs and want to make a pet of him, just be sure he has a little cage all to himself, because if you put two in the same cage, the stronger just naturally eats the weaker, prayerful attitude notwithstanding. However, it is kind of fun to watch him tilt his little head to the side, as he watches you approach with a tasty tidbit, like a wriggly mealworm, or a piece of raw vegetable, or a piece of raw beef. You can even teach him to take it right from your fingers. And he'll show his good drinking manners by sipping slyly and slickly from a teaspoon.

Actually, he likes to eat insects better than any other food. He hunts by sitting on flower stems or around the outer leaves of plants, waiting for an unwary meal to flit or flutter by, crawl or creep near, or hop and hobble closer. And the way he catches a delicious ladybug or groovy grasshopper is to quickly reach out with his two front legs, which are really two pincers with little, little needles along the edges, then clasp, clutch, crunch, and kill!

While he's waiting for dinner to be served, he sits with those two pincer legs up in front of him as though he's praying, and in an insect way he probably is, praying for quick service, that is. It's this posture that gives him the name, *praying mantis.* Of course, many folks spell it "preying mantis" and that seems to fit too. He has another nickname which doesn't seem to suit too well though, often being called a "soothsayer." Makes him sound like the astrologer of the bug world.

Orville once said to Wilbur, "It'll never get off the ground," and some smart alecks say the same thing when they look at this heavy-bodied, green and brown, flesh eater. But fly he can, and in a manner that's almost startling. He's been seen swinging his merry way at the observation tower atop the Empire State Building, and that's a long way up for insects to soar, especially without rocket takeoffs!

Comes autumn, and Mama Mantis lays about 200 eggs in a sort of sticky blob that hardens pretty quickly into a walnut-sized mass. It's usually found attached to the stem of some plant. Then in the springtime, all the eggs hatch at once, and 200 little buggers drop to the ground and quickly scamper off. They have to scamper quickly too, because if they don't, some of their quicker brothers and sisters just gobble them up, for, you see, just as soon as they're born, they're entirely on their own and more than capable of getting their own breadbaskets filled. If you can't beat 'em, eat 'em!

HE DIGS MOUNTAINS

CHAS. HERZOG III

Mole

Fred Allen once told of an editor who came into the office every morning and found a molehill on his desk. It was his job to make a mountain out of it by lunchtime. Well, mountains may be difficult to build, but apparently mole hills are easy to come by----especially if you're a mole.

Moles are sensational diggers, admirably equipped for the job. They have sensitive noses that feel for the soft spot in the soil, and short, powerful forelegs with strong claws at the end, perfect for churning into the good earth. They practically gallop along, excavating a tunnel the length of a football field in less than twenty four hours. Which seems as easy as eating raw oysters with chopsticks! For them, living is like farming—you have to start over again every morning. They must eat their own weight in insects and worms every day so that they can have enough energy to dig for insects and worms every day. Do you dig, Man?

Their body shape is perfect for the kind of life they lead. Tapered to a point at either end, no neck, short strong legs, and, because they spend almost all their lives underground, eyes that are about as useful as knotholes in a lumberyard fire. About all they can see is the difference between night and day, and for the shift they work, what's the difference? .

Moles live in the more temperate regions of the Old World and the New World, never making it too far to the north where the ground freezes to a great depth, or to the tropics where the earth is too dry for their underground food to live. The strange-looking little creature, the star-nosed mole pictured here, loves to live in damp fields and marshes of northwestern North America, where he helps keep the soil fertile.

Old Star-nosed could win a prize for making the funniest face while trying to imitate Cyrano de Bergerac. The gimmick that gives this animal his name is made up of very sensitive, pink-colored feelers, twenty-two of them, arranged in a nice convenient disc on the tip of the nose. But what good is a gimmick like that unless you're going to a masquerade party disguised as an emery wheel? Actually the feelers on the disc are somewhat like the whiskers on a cat, sensors to help Mister Mole dig his hole, as he feels his way underground or underwater, to pick up sounds of insects or worms. Ah, yes, the nose knows.

Few people have ever really seen a mole, especially the Stellar Prosbosciced one, for they rarely come above ground except in the springtime, which is their mating season. So if you see a little furry, six or seven inch long, almost blind, pugnacious, hard-working voracious, mouse-like animal fooling around with another amorous little creature who looks just the same, it's not only springtime, it's time to send a wedding present, such as a giftwrapped can of worms!

THE SNAKE SWALLOWER

Mongoose

It is written: "There's no way of knowing how many heroes originally intended to be cowards but ran the wrong way!" And there's now way of knowing how many mongooses lost the fight to the cobra, but the odds are that this little, long bodied, weasel-like creature gave a darned good account of himself. The mongoose, star of Rudyard Kipling's famous story in the *Jungle Book,* whose maiden name was Rikki-Tikki-Tavi, was a native of India, but he has many relatives in both Asia and Africa, and killing snakes is only one of his habits.

The mongoose, a name which comes from the Sanskrit, is brave, cocky, quick, and numerous, and one of the most effective natural enemies of mice, rats, birds, and scorpions, and while he's not a complete dummy, and really doesn't look for a fight, he will, if the tiny pangs of hunger goad him, take on one of the most deadly of enemies, the snake whose venom kills over 25,000 people a year, the Indian cobra.

The experienced mongoose with his sharp reflexes will bob and weave, dodge and feint, move and maneuver so that the snake will strike, and hopefully miss. Everytime the snake strikes and misses and lies on the ground fully extended, the wily mongoose dashes in and tries to sink his sharp little teeth into the cobra's head; when he does, the party's over but the banquet's just beginning. The mongoose starts to eat, and eat, and eat, and eat. He swallows the snake's head first, poison glands and all, and if he can't finish a ten foot long meal all in one sitting, he'll just lie down, sleep awhile, and then get up and finish swallowing. And you thought you did well with a foot-long hotdog!

Of course, you can't win them all, and when this two foot long animal miscalculates a smidgin and gets a full load of venom, the legend is that he hightails it into the jungle and eats magic herbs or roots and then the poison has no effect. You might just as well believe that cats wear pajamas and meat balls bounce like tennis balls. However, some mongooses seem to survive even after being bitten, and there's the stubborn theory that the constant eating of snakes gives him a degree of immunity against the poison. Which to me is like getting shot with a .22 several times so that you can withstand the blast of a .45.

This herky-jerky little devil is more active during the day than at night, which makes the fact that his piercing little eyes are bright red, difficult to explain. He has the habit of stopping frequently, cocking his head, raising one foot, and listening for a glistening second for anything that might eat or be eaten, then hurrying and scurrying along. If he's cornered he can climb a tree, but he doesn't do that too often. He'd rather run. Me too.

The mongoose has a disposition like an untipped waiter, but in spite of this, if he's taken young enough, and treated kindly, he'll grow up to be a most remarkable and tractable pet, living cheek by jowl with cats or dogs, and keeping your house free of rats—to say nothing of snakes. The only thing no one's ever been able to teach a mongoose is to leave the poultry alone. He digs chickens the most, the duck has no luck, and the goose hangs loose.

CYRANO THE SIMIAN

CHAS. HERZOG III

Proboscis Monkey

Cyrano, the long-nosed gallant from Bergerac, gloried in his nose, claiming that it indicated a great being, genial, courteous, intellectual, virile, and courageous. Poetic Cyrano even described his big beak as a crag, a cape, a veritable peninsula whose colors did not fade in the sun, and when he smoked a cigar, the neighbors asked if his chimney was on fire! Jimmy Durante, the modern day Cyrano, merely claimed that he couldn't raise a moustache, because it wouldn't grow in the shade! Well, the animal kingdom also has its personality with the big honker. No, not the elephant, not a tapir, and not a rhino. None other than the proboscis monkey, certainly one of the homeliest primates in the world.

The simian Cyrano really has a remarkable nose, sometimes hanging well below his chin. An ideal ad for a box of Kleenex. Not only his nose long and large, but also quite mobile with a furrow right down the center so that he looks as though he actually has two noses, sort of a parkerhouse roll with nostrils. He doesn't chatter like other monkeys, but rather seems to take a deep breath, and then, in a long drawn out manner, "honks" or "kee-honks" with a bass resonance, as though he's had laryngitis for a month.

Old Big Nose lives in Borneo and is pretty big as monkeys go, attaining a length of 30 inches, sporting a reddish-colored coat tastefully touched with gray on his lower limbs and lower back----a veritable fashion plate of monkeydom. Strangely, like most Old World monkeys, his tail doesn't have the ability to grasp things and help him swing from trees, where he spends most of his time. But the tree that makes him happy is the tree near the water for he knows how to swim and seems to enjoy it. And how about this, the monkey uses the "dog paddle." Maybe he calls it the "Borneo Crawl" and adapted it from Australia. Anyhow, if he's ever fired upon, he merely dives underwater and swims to safety. After all what good is having a big nose if you can't smell trouble with it?

The Malay folks call him *blanda*, the natives' word for "Dutchman," which may make the monkey happy, but the Netherlanders aren't too thrilled with the little nickname, I'll bet. The proboscis monkey eats no meat, just fruit and the simian equivalent of vegetables, travels in small troops, and loves to sit for hours, very quiet and very calmly on a branch, contemplating his navel, his fate, and his startling resemblance to Tiny Tim. I wonder, if he had a choice, would he have picked this nose?

CHAS. HERZOG III

Moose

The plural of *blouse* is *blice,* the plural of *mouse* is *meese,* and the singular of moose is one of the largest mammals on the North American continent, the giant of the deer family, the monumental moose. If the camel is an animal that was put together by a committee, then the moose is an animal that was put together by Walt Disney, the Jolly Green Giant, and a nearsighted patternmaker.

His legs are too long for his body, his shoulders belong on a hulking linebacker, his neck is as short and thick as a cluster of fire hydrants, and he has lips that would make it easy for him to seal a letter----after it was in the mailbox. He can't bend down and graze on short grass unless he kneels, and he can't drink unless he wades out in the water up to his belly. And you think you look funny?

Actually, however, his long legs make it easy for him to reach the twigs and leaves of the willow trees, and even easier to travel through thick underbrush and fallen timber that would be impossible for a shorter legged creature to clamber over and around. He also has a sweet tooth when it comes to one of his favorite foods, the water lily. He'll even wade out into water over his head and submarine it, just to get a succulent water lily. Luckily he's a vegetarian, or else fish would have still another formidable foe!

The bull moose, from the political party of the same name, has antlers that can weigh up to 60 pounds and be as large as 6 feet across, which is in keeping with an animal that oftimes grows up to be 8 feet tall at the shoulder and weigh close to 1,800 pounds. It's the Alaskan moose we're talking about here. There are four varieties of North American moose and three kinds of European moose, which they call *elk,* over there.

Old Man Moose has a tremendous nose, which would be tough if he suffered from postnasal drip; his ears are large, the better to hear you with my dear; and his floppy, upper lip is ideal for slurping up foliage. His head is long, about a size 69-7/8, long oval, while his coat is coarse, long, and blackish brown in color, with gray tones on his underside. If they ever held a beauty contest for moose, no one would win. As if that isn't enough, he has a bag-like growth of skin that hangs from his throat, like a burglar's tool kit, that's called a "bell."

If he looks like that, why do hunters insist on hunting him, putting him on the endangered species list? Must be because of his size, his power, and the danger of getting close to him, although most hunters use rifles that shoot five miles and then send for help. Some danger!

The moose isn't a really sociable animal, he doesn't travel in herds, although I have heard of Moose conventions in Atlantic City, complete with wild parties and joy buzzers, but the big moose, the four-legged variety, is a pretty solitary creature and even sticks to one mate. When one bull fights for the lady of his choice it's one heckuva battle with trees getting slashed, ground getting torn up, and the other forest inhabitants getting out of the way. No one seems to know how long they live in the wild, but in captivity they rarely live longer than two years. They can't stand the pace of our society, I guess. Who can?

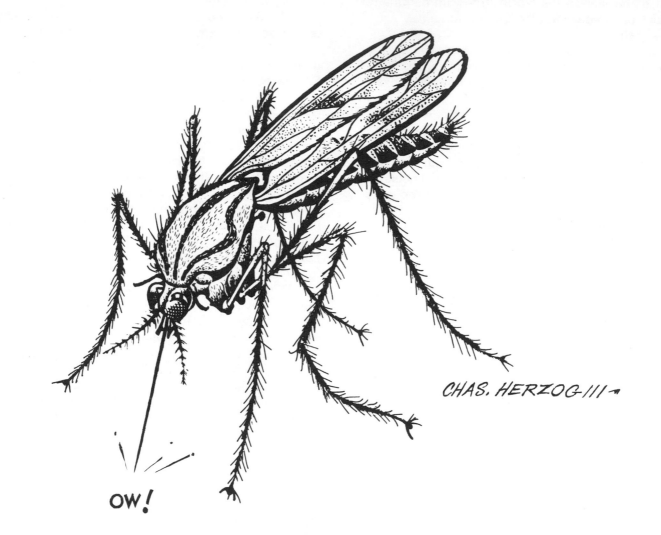

Mosquito

There's some good in everything. Even a stopped clock is right twice a day, and there's even some good in an insect that causes much suffering in animals and humans. For instance, the pesky mosquito, who's responsible for the spread of malaria, yellow fever, dengue, encephalomyelitis, filariasis, and sleepless nights, is important as a food source for other insects, birds, animals, and fish.

It's interesting to note that only the female mosquito does the biting, while the only vice of the chauvinistic male is chasing female mosquitoes, which immediately shows that the male isn't all bad. Mosquitoes seem to bite mostly at night, that is, the species of mosquito that is called the "house" or "rain barrel" mosquito, the one that can squeeze through the tiniest opening in the tightest screen. This annoying insect is a night feeder, and so when you turn off the light you're turning on the dinner bell.

There are approximately 3,000 kinds of mosquitoes and on some hot summer nights they all seem to be holding a convention on your campsite, singing their little high-pitched songs of delight as they dive bomb your tender skin. The truth of the matter is that they don't sing at all, it's just the whirring of their devilish wings. Ah, but how do they find you in the dark, you ask, and the answer is . . . easy. They seem to have radar-like sensors in their feathery antennaes and a sense of "smell" in the hairs of their legs, and with these James Bond gimmicks they can zero in on their targets by following the heat waves and sensing the body odors given off by the victim. An unkempt hippie could drive a self respecting "skeeter" bananas.

And if you think life is short, just consider the male mosquito . . . his average life span is only eight days. Two days after he's born, he dates and mates a female mosquito—in midair, which maybe explains why he only lives eight days. The female, however, has 30 days of life before she heads for that big Raid can in the sky, laying her eggs, about 100 at a time, on the surface of water. From the beginning of spring, till the end of fall, about fifteen generations of mosquitoes are born, which, if left unmolested, would result in over sixty billion, himming, zinging, stinging pests. We could be up to our eyeballs in mosquitoes in just nine short months, and so, you see, control of the pesty little insects is not really a luxury, but a darned important necessity.

The female never wears shoes, 'cause then you'd know immediately when she settled on your skin for a real Bloody Mary. What she does have, however, are friction pads on the bottom of her feet which stick like fishhooks dipped in glue on top of molasses. Then she unlimbers her hypodermic torture tool, a marvelously engineered hollow drill sharper than a well honed scalpel, that stimulates the flow of blood and easily penetrates the toughest skin. She turns on a little pump in her head and starts siphoning up the blood, sometimes sucking up three to four times her own weight, and that's known as really putting the bite on a friend.

And one last little note . . . the kind of clothes you wear sometimes determines whether or not you'll get bitten. Experiments have proven that ten times more mosquitoes bite people in dark clothing than in light clothing, so if you're going on a safari to mosquito-laden areas, wear something light. The material most avoided—shiny white satin and black silk—is guaranteed to make a mosquito happier than if she'd just passed a screen test!

Ocelot

Someone once said that cows are bitter and neurotic, because, like taxpayers, they're tired of being milked. And the ocelot is also somewhat on the bitter side of things and not only becoming neurotic, but scarce, as hunters unmercifully chase them down for their beautiful fur. I sure wish corduroy coats would come into style, or that someone would find that fur coats cause warts, bad breath, and flat feet.

One of the reasons that I'm so fond of the ocelot is that, like most actors, he's a night creature. He's at home in the deep gloom of the South American jungle, never leaving his den until all the evening light has faded. The darker the night, the happier the ocelot. Even pale and wan moonlight makes him as nervous as a man with a wooden leg in a forest fire.

He spends most of his time on the ground, but he seems to like climbing trees every now and then, especially if there's a nice, fat bird's nest loaded with eggs to snack on, and if bird's nests aren't too plentiful, he'll settle for a leaping lizard, a skulking squirrel, or a slippery snake. Opossums and rodents of any sort that he can catch and kill, make up his diet, and it must agree with him, because I've never seen or heard of a fat or overweight ocelot. He usually eats three to five pounds of meat at a time, and with the price of meat nowadays, it's a good thing he has his own butcher shop.

The ocelot can run like a fox and think like a secretary. He's very difficult to catch, knowing instinctively how to backtrack and doublecross his trail, and nearly always has a nice comfortable rocky cave or hollow tree for a home. And talk about a nifty homemaker! Well, sir, the ocelot has the strange habit of chewing twigs, dry grass, underbrush, and stuff like-that-there until it's all soft and pliable, and then lining his cave with great care so that the bedding rivals a peachy Posturepedic. You might say that the creature, indeed, digs his creature comfort, and is very "chewsy" about where he lives.

The ocelot's kittens are nearly always born in September and October, which makes most ocelots Libras. They're born almost always as twins (maybe they ought to be Geminis), and have their eyes tightly closed when they come into our imperfect world. If they're taken young enough, they'll become tame and gentle pets, but a full-grown ocelot has a disposition like a toothless beaver in the petrified forest and is not recommended as a house pet.

From the tip of his nose to the tip of his tail, an ocelot measures close to four feet long, with soft, short, and beautiful fur to make him one of the most beautiful cats in the world today. His markings are a medley of spots, stripes, and black rings set against light buff, and if we could only add a bullet-proof vest, we might keep this fancy feline around a little longer.

THE EIGHT-LEGGED LAGGARD

Octopus

There's a small and smiling, potbellied philosopher of Greek origin named Demetrius Butsicaris who sits around with a pencil between his toes (for footnotes) and has the answer to most questions, and so I asked him if he'd ever seen an eight-legged animal. *"Okto,"* he replied, "means 'eight,' and *pous* means 'foot'." The Greeks had a word for it, for indeed octopus means "eight-legged," and that's the much maligned mollusk we'll take a look at here.

Contrary to the terrifying reputation of this devilfish, the octopus is actually timid and retiring and deathly afraid of anything larger than he is. And while there are unconfirmed reports of sensational monsters that measure more than a 100 feet from the tip of one tentacle to the tip of another, it is rare to find one larger than 3 feet across. There are over 100 varieties and some are so small that full grown they could fit into a thimble, and still have enough room left over for 69 grains of salt and a drama critic's heart.

The movement of an octopus is fascinating, and not near as fast as legend has it. Matter of fact, he moves slower than two weeks when you're on a diet, but he does have two methods of getting from here to there. One is jet-propulsion, where he opens his gills, draws in water and then squirts it out through a sort-of exhaust pipe which zips him ahead two or three yards per squirt. Shorter trips are for little squirts. The other way he moves is to sort of toe-dance, or rather tentacle-dance, on the tips of his tenacles, just flowing along like a big blob of blah.

One of the most amazing things about this enthralling animal is that he has the ability to change color at will: if he's on yellow sand, he becomes pale yellow; on rocks he becomes red or dark brown; on seaweed, a bright green; and if put upon a tartan plaid, he mottles up and looks like an eight-legged kilt, honest. If an enemy, like the ferocious Moray eel, frightens him, he turns pale, just as you and I, and if he's really terrified, he'll flash from color to color, like a hippie in a strong solution of soap.

For hundreds of years scientists thought that the "ink" an octopus squirted was merely a smoke screen so that enemies couldn't find him, but recent tests have shown that it really goofs up the ability of some of his sharp-toothed predators to find him by the sense of smell. The "ink" has no effect on human skin, and does no harm to fishes swimming through it. Maybe it's also for old-fashioned fountain pens that still write under water.

The octopus is one of the ugliest creatures in the world, by human standards. To another octopus maybe he looks like Rock Hudson. And there's slim evidence of an octopus ever attacking a human being, but there's little doubt that if a man attacked one of the larger species he could be grabbed by one or more of the eight suction-cupped arms and drown before he could free himself.

Ollie the Octopus has a problem getting enough to eat and spends most of the night on the prowl, spending the daylight hours holed up in a niche in the rocks. Fish ordinarily are too fast for him to catch, and so he eats crabs and other small shellfish, using his parrot-like beak to crack the shells. Strangely enough, his eyes, which have no lids, are almost as highly developed as ours. His five senses are the same as ours, and as a result he can be tamed quite easily and with a little thoughtful care could make an interesting pet.

You might even get a boy octopus pet and a girl octopus pet, let them fall in love, and then watch them swim into a romantic sunset, hand in hand, hand in hand, hand in hand, hand in hand.

Orangutan

In the old days they used to call the region west of the Mississippi, the "Wild and Wooly West," because the women were wild and the men wore woolies----which is what made the women wild! The late, great P. T. Barnum took one look at a wild and wooly, powerful, long armed ape, with its brick red hair, and called it "wild, man, wild." He was looking at an orangutan, and since the orangutan comes from Borneo, it was billed as the "Wild Man of Borneo," which seems fair enough.

The average male orang stands a little over four feet high with an armspread that can reach 7-1/2 feet from fingertip to fingertip, and weigh as much as 300 pounds, which would make a ready-made, off the rack suit pretty hard to come by. Only the heaviest, most luxuriant, densest part of the forest is inhabited by our henna-rinsed ape, who swings by his great, long powerful arms from limb to limb and tree to tree. Not a hurried kind of swinger, he can still travel faster then a man can run over the forest floor below.

The natives of Borneo and Sumatra say that the orangutan has no real enemies, and that only a crocked crocodile or a pixilated python is stupid enough to attack him. An attacking crocodile, for instance, faces the brute strength of the orang, who pulls open the croc's mouth and just tears out its tongue and throat, while the python merely faces the great jaw and formidable canine tooth of the orang as he bites the great snake in two. Sure wish he was my congressman.

He may not look it, but the orangutan is a cheerful and intelligent animal, sort of a well adjusted suburbanite, whose family life seems to occupy most of his time, with several small mouths to feed and one big mouth to listen to. The orang lives mostly on unripe fruit, especially a large, spiny, pulpy fruit called the *durian*. He doesn't get up in the morning until the sun has dried the dew from the leaves, and then he spends the rest of the day just feeding the family and his fat, wattled face.

The night life in the jungle is sort of on the dull side for an orangutan, and so he just builds a rude kind of platform of branches and leaves, a temporary shelter that he may use just once, and climbs into his nest like a great, hairy, short legged, wingless bird and sleeps the night away. The nest is rarely more than twenty-five feet from the ground, so that it's not exposed too much and not too windy; and during the rainy season, the "Wild Man of Borneo" simply covers himself with a nice thick blanket of leaves.

Ah, laugh and the world laughs with you----snore and you sleep in the guest nest.

Osprey

As Percy Q. Dovetonsil once said, "Show me a man with both feet on the ground----and I'll show you a man who can't get his pants off!" Then, show me a fierce creature who loves solitude, flies like the air was made for him, a creature who's magnificently adopted for the kind of life he leads, a creature called an *osprey*----and I'll show you a hawk, for indeed, an osprey is a hawk.

Hawks are related to eagles, condors, falcons, kites, harriers, and vultures, which is sort of like marrying the devil's daughter and then having your in-laws move in with you. All these birds of prey have powerful wings, slashing beaks, hooked talons, and sensational eyesight, and range in size from hardly larger than a sparrow to the ten foot wingspread of the high flying condor. They're birds of a feather, but they don't necessarily flock together.

If there's anything that'll make a fish more nervous than a Friday, it would have to be an osprey, a large bird with a wingspan of over five feet and a length of about two feet. And what a fisherman he is! Izaak Walton would chortle in glee to see him glide gracefully in a long, easy wheeling manner, hawkeyes zeroed in as he glides silently and slickly over the water. When he spots a delectable and unsuspecting fish, he just sort of hovers for a few moments and then---slam, bang, alakazam! Down he dives, hitting the water like a feathered, flying muscle---the jig is up, the fish is out, and daddy doesn't have to go a-hunting for awhile.

The osprey has a few tricks up his plumed pinions too. For instance, his feathers are packed extremely close together on his breast and underparts, making a compact shock absorber when he slams into the water in a headlong dive. Can you imagine taking a bellywhopper everytime you wanted to eat, and having no padding? In no time at all you'd have a chest like the inside of a spoon. And how about holding a wriggling, squirming, slippery, sliding fish, when you decided to take off again? It'd be like shooting marbles with freshly peeled grapes, and so old Mama Nature to the rescue once again. The osprey has long, curved, very sharp claws to slash, clutch, clasp, and hold. The only one who can take a fish away from him is a lazy eagle, who may, on occasion, hijack an unwary osprey, just sort of swoop down on him, start a little ruckus and snatch the fish when the osprey fights back.

The nest is a pretty large affair and more often than not it's built in a dead tree. Why a dead tree no one seems to know, and every so often—when the trees haven't died fast enough, I guess—he'll build the nest right on the ground. Mama Osprey usually lays three or four eggs at a time, beautifully blotched with brown, so pretty it seems that in the British Isles egg fanciers collected them in such great numbers that the poor bird became extinct there.

Ospreys breed in all sorts of places, like happy humans, but their favorite places seem to be coastal regions. However, he's often found wheeling and dealing around large rivers or lakes. His head is white and so is his underside, while the upper parts are dark brown, and the female is usually larger than the male. When he's henpecked, he really gets pecked!

A PARROT WITH A NOSE JOB?

Owl

Some smart aleck comedian, when he first saw an owl, was heard to remark, "Why, it's nothing but a parrot with a nose job!" Of course, that isn't true. Our friend the owl is in a class by himself. A most valuable bird from man's point of view too, in that he is sure death to harmful rodents and insects. When he whips down on a shrew, a mouse, or other small mammal, it's all over but the eating.

For many years, people associated the owl with the hawk, but their similarity was mainly in the manner of their swooping and preying and that's all. Actually owls are related to another group of birds whose metabolism is adjusted to nighttime living, the strangely named birds called *nightjars* and *goatsuckers*. When a hawk sweeps down on a hapless victim, his strong wings whirr and wail, but when an owl starts into his dive of death, he's got a great advantage. His wing feathers are fringed with down and as a result his deadly descent is muffled and as silent as a kitten on cotton. His bill is powerful; his feet like grappling hooks.

Something interesting about these hooting, screeching, or wailing creatures, is that they generally gobble their prey whole. Why waste time chewing? And then after a while they bring the subject up again. They regurgitate undigestible bones and fur in the form of small pellets, which then clutter up their roosts and nests, somewhat reminiscent of a sloppy bachelor's pad after a wild Saturday night.

Owls are active at night and so there's no need for bright plumage. Usually they're duller than the laying of a cornerstone at a dental floss factory, but what they lack in brightness they make up for in subtle shading and intricate feather patterns. The feature that's most associated with owls, however, is the eye. It's big, it's round, and unlike most other birds, it's on the front of his flat face, which gives him that which is called *binocular vision*, the same as yours and mine. The size of the eye is necessarily large to be able to gather the weak light available at night, while his hearing is probably the best in the bird world, almost sharp enough to hear grass growing.

In many birds of prey, the female is larger than the male, and the owl follows this pattern too. Just why this is no one seems to really know. Maybe Mama Owl wears the feather pants in the family. Owls usually live in hollow trees and lay white eggs that are much rounder than other birds', and when hatched the youngsters not only have a voracious appetite, and vicious disposition, but become mature at a much slower rate than other feathered flyers, but then, they seem to live longer—one great horned owl in a zoo reaching the ripe old age of sixty-eight.

Some owls are even pugnacious enough to wallop the daylights out of an eagle, taking over the eagle's nest. Some owls are ferocious enough to clobber a hawk, knock off a rabbit, a hen, a skunk, or a domestic cat. Some owls, like the barred owl, even have the cannibalistic habit of feeding on their smaller owl cousins. Some owls, like the snowy owl, are not only white, but won't join the union, and hunt during the daylight hours. Some owls are over two feet long and there's even an owl that's no bigger than a sparrow and lives in a giant cactus.

Just why the owl is associated with wisdom we're not really sure, because studies have shown that what once passed for wisdom and mystery is really nothing more than stupidity and lethargy. But the ancient Greeks believed the owl was wise; in the Middle Ages the English thought the owl was wise; and in our time, well, there's the Owl and the Pussycat.

LOVES ORANGE JUICE, HATES PUBLICITY

Giant Panda

It looks like a bear, it acts like a clown, it's rarer than a day in June or a parking space in December, and it's related to the raccoon. It's also one of the best known animals in the world, although outside of China, only four are in captivity. One in London and one in Moscow and two in the U.S. of A.---and by this time you've guessed it's the giant panda we're talking about.

He's most certainly bearlike in appearance, about 6 feet long and weighs up to 300 pounds. A great big, roly-poly beast who seems to be wearing black stockings that look like they're fastened to a black shoulder harness; with a huge, creamy-white head sporting black "ear mufs"; and black circles around the eyes that make him look as though he'd been on a three-day binge. An amusing looking animal made popular by toy makers 'round the world.

The giant panda lives a secluded life high in the mountain fastnesses of China and Tibet, haunting the almost impenetrable forests of bamboo-----and bamboo pulp shoots and leaves are what he eats mostly. It's just too bad that he can't eat his way past the Chinese Bamboo Curtain or we might know more about this interesting creature. Matter of fact, no one in the western world even heard of the panda before 1869, and the first one to ever be brought to the United States was in 1937, receiving more publicity than a movie star's escapades. Unfortunately he didn't live too long in captivity---maybe he didn't like the publicity.

He's flatfooted and lumbers along much like a bear, yet he's a darned good tree climber and pretty agile for an ungainly looking giant ball of fur. And while he eats bamboo almost exclusively in the wild, using his great flat molars to grind and crush the bamboo, in captivity he seems to thrive on vegetables, milk, and cod liver oil, cereals, and other vitamin supplements. And because he's so big, the folks in the know guess that in the wilds of his homeland he has to eat at least ten to twelve hours every day just to keep going. Oddly enough the few in captivity show a strong love of orange juice so don't be surprised if we see him making a citrus growers' commercial in the near future.

On each of the panda's front paws is a pad, which he can use in a most interesting manner, something like a thumb, in bringing food to his mouth. Sometimes he uses both front paws like hands, much like a squirrel, or maybe he'll just lie on his back, piling the food on his belly before starting a meal . . . mighty handy place when reading in bed. He can also hold a stalk of celery in his paw and chomp off a mouthful at a time, a pretty clever maneuver for an animal without fingers and no table manners.

Since the panda is so rare in the western world no one really knows just what kind of personality he really has. The ones in the zoos are delightful clowns we're told, acting like furry buffoons of the slapstick variety. No one really knows whether they hibernate or not, whether they give birth to more than one cub at a time, how they defend themselves, or whether, as some keepers describe them, they're friendly and affectionate. Some keepers say they're quite irritable and aggressive and that, like some television actors, they grow ill-tempered and sullen with age. And since he rarely gets out of Red China, maybe his varied moods reflect the ups and downs of Chinese politics.

CHAS. HERZOG III

Pangolin

If time heals all wounds, why does a bellybutton look like it does? And if all mammals grow an insulating fur or hair, why does this four-legged pine cone called the *pangolin*, have reptile-like scales?

The answer is that the pangolin is unlike any other mammal, an isolated survivor from the past, not related to anything living today. He acquired his strange and interesting characteristics only sixty million years ago-----and hasn't changed since. He hasn't changed any more than the shape of the earth, which we, at times, admit is mighty square.

He isn't a lizard, a diminutive dinosaur, a pine cone or an armadillo. He has the scales of a reptile, the living habits of an aardvark, the tree climbing ability of a raccoon, and the stomach of a six year old at the circus. He's the one, the only, the pangolin.

The outstanding characteristic of this three to four foot long creature is indeed his scales—but he does have hair too! The hair grows between the scales and on his underside as well. Sometimes, on old timers, the belly hair is worn completely away and the tough skin is exposed, like a Helena Rubenstein drop-out. The scales, however, are unique, differing from snakes only in that he doesn't shed his skin. When one of the horny, overlapping plates wears out, the precocious pangolin merely grows another one. And that's as handy as having ears when you wear bifocals.

The other unique feature of the creature is his digestive system. While it is true that, like anteaters and aardvarks, he doesn't have a tooth in his head, he actually does have teeth----in his stomach! Which obviously poses a pretty good problem for the dentist. Here's how it works: He first tears open the ant or termite hill with his powerful and enormous front claws, and dangles his long, slender, sticky, eighteen-inch tongue into the cluster of insects and merely slurps and swallows. The phenomenal stomach then grinds at the front, adds acids in the middle, and then actually "chews" the food with horny knobs that look like teeth, before gurgling the entire unsavory mixture into the intestines. Bromo, anyone?

The pangolin is surprisingly agile. He can run fast, climb quickly and surely, and hang by his tail. He protects himself by rolling up, which is where he actually get his name. You see, the Malay word *peng-goling* means "roller." And I suppose if he were religious he might be called a *holy roller.* Anyhow, the seven species of pangolin are found in Africa and southeastern Asia.

It is also interesting to note that the baby pangolin rides securely on momma's back by digging his claws into the scales at the base of his mother's tail. That way, when momma is threatened, she can stop abruptly, curl up quickly, cover the baby completely, and present an almost invulnerable ball of scales to her enemies. How many times a day do you wish you could do the same?

ROCKING IT WITH THE PENGUIN

CHAS. HERZOG III

Penguin

He waddles, he weaves, he waves, he looks like the headwaiter at a midget restaurant, and in his spare time he poses for pictures on a cigarette package. He'd never make it in the army—his feet are too flat. We call him a *penguin,* the naturalists call him a *Sphenisciforme,* which means "short winged bird," a bird that doesn't fly and walks as though he'd ridden a horse all day.

The contrast between this jolly, whimiscal, potbellied bird and his natural environment is startling. The dreary wastes and the barren landscape just don't seem to go with this comical, wobbly-legged creature. However, not all penguins live in the south polar regions, only two of the seventeen species eke out an existence down there, the Emperor and the Adelie penguins. They live on the Antarctic continent. The other no-necked midgets live on islands and barren coasts as far north as Australia. Even in South America the chill waters of the Humboldt Current allow this baggypants top banana of the bird world to live around Peru and the Galápagos Islands, which to most folks is as surprising as getting down on your knees to propose and seeing another fellow hiding under the couch.

Penguins range in size from twelve inches high to more than three feet tall and vary in weight from four pounds to ninety pounds, but they all have pretty much the same "human" characteristics—an upright stance, flat feet, a short tail, and a rude gawking stare. Ah, but they can swim like a berserk beaver, using a powerful overhand stroke of their flipper-like wings, diving and leaping as they cleave the water like the great and graceful porpoise. One of the funniest things they do is sliding on their bellies over ice and drifts when they're in a hurry. Sort of like a built-in Flexible Flyer with waterproof feathers for runners.

When warmer weather sets in and the snows begin to melt, the petulant penguin has to raise the level of the nest. He does this by using pebbles as a foundation, which shows that he's not a complete birdbrain. And just to show that he's a very practical animal, the male penguin courts his lady love by presenting her with pebbles, laying them at her feet—one at a time—for her close inspection. Can't you just hear one popular swinger talking to her jealous girl friend, "Louise, you'll never believe the size of the rock Harry gave me?"

HE'LL SQUEAL ON YOU . . .

CHAS. HERZOG-III

Pig

Al Blanchard, celebrated former columnist for the *Detroit News,* and the fellow who gives advice to people with bald heads (which is akin to Eddie Fisher giving advice to Richard Burton), recently wrote about a much maligned animal, an animal whose ancestry dates back to prehistoric times, an animal far more intelligent than the dog, the horse, or the cat, an animal whose use includes everything but the grunt-----and we're working on that.

We're talking about the pig, of course, an animal you can eat for breakfast, roast for holidays, and call people you don't like. Strangely enough, even though the pig loves to wallow in the mud, he's essentially a clean animal. He doesn't even over-eat, never worries about Metrecal, and makes a heckuva nice pet. Animal trainers find him not only relatively easy to train, but lovable as well. About the only thing they haven't taught him to do is say "Oinkel."

There are over twenty breeds of pigs today, and in the wild, if given a choice of where to live, they pick a warm and temperate region. They can swim, but they can't climb trees. They're sociable animals and love company. They really enjoy rooting for tubers and truffles, but they won't turn their snout up at any other delectable tidbit, whether it's animal or vegetable, although they have a little trouble with minerals---rocks are a little hard to digest.

Years ago, certain religions discovered that pig meat sometimes was dangerous to eat and so the pig was forbidden in the diet, which didn't make the pig too angry at all. The reason for the danger was a little-known parasite called *trichinella* which causes trichinosis, a deadly disease of the intestine and the muscles, which man needs like a barracuda needs Polident.

Way back when Barnacle Bill the Sailor was a cabin boy, salt pork was the most important meat item in a sailing ship's larder. Not only did it last longer than any other kind of meat, but it was both cheap and plentiful. Plentiful because porkers are great breeders. (We told you they were very sociable!) Three litters of young are not uncommon, with between eight and twenty-two to the litter, which is kind of tough on Mama Pig, although she has more faucets, spigots, or nipples than any other kind of animal—as many as twenty-eight, and that makes mama at lunchtime busier than a mosquito in a nudist colony.

If you get a chance, take a close look at a pig's snout, one of the most remarkable instruments in the animal world. It's tougher than leather noodles, actually a combination of bulldozer and steam shovel. It can lift, push, dig, and break through rough brush with an ease that's hard to believe. The muzzle is flexible, the blunt plate at the end of the snout is reinforced by gristle that's attached to the skull, and the whole thing is capable of withstanding a rifle shot at close range. (And you thought Superman was tough!) The teeth are kept pretty sharp as the upper teeth hone themselves against the lower teeth, and that's the whole tooth and nothing but. So think before you sell our friend, the porcine one, short. He's more than formidable. He can be a menace if not to life, at least to limb!

HE'S NO BATHING BUDDY

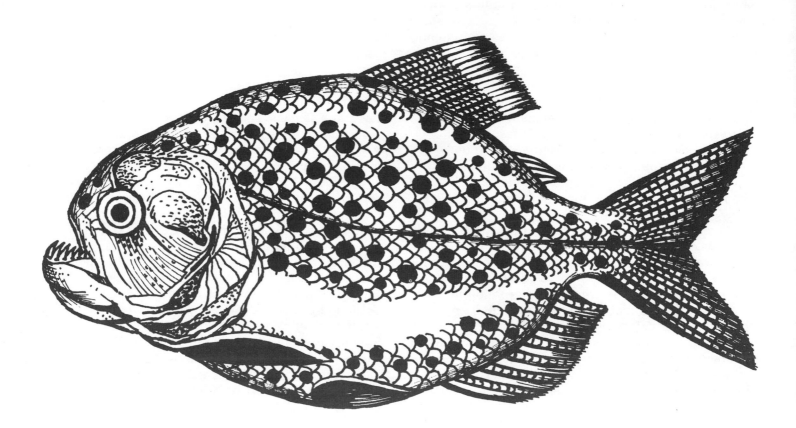

Piranha

It's non-habit forming if you stick your head in a bucket of water three times and only pull it out twice. It's also not recommended that you bob for apples in a crocodile pool, or enter a swimming meet with a tiger shark—all of these little endeavors are guaranteed to put an end to the problem of keeping your hair in and your teeth from falling out. However, there's something that's even more dangerous, and that's swimming through a school of one of the most savage little fish in the world, the piranha.

More human beings have been killed by the piranha than any other fish! No creature is too large or too powerful to prevent its being attacked by these slashing, flashing fish. Of course, only one little fish could just nip and snack, but large numbers of piranha are capable of stripping the flesh from a 150 pound animal in less than two minutes, leaving only a skeleton, picked as clean as a surgical thread.

There are four dangerous kinds of piranhas, the largest of which only gets about ten inches long, with teeth that would make a dentist gleefully warm up his X-ray machine, razor sharp, triangular and plentiful. Their jaw muscles are strong enough to bite an ordinary fishhook in two, and the larger ones can rip out an olive-sized piece of flesh in each bite. Like the shark he goes slightly berserk when blood is in the water, wildly snapping and tearing, ripping and slashing in all directions, even attacking his own kind in his frenetic frenzy, which is probably why the Spaniards named this dangerous critter the *caribe,* which means, appropriately enough, "cannibal!"

This fresh water fury lives in South American streams that drain into the Atlantic, like the Amazon, Sao Fransisco, Orinoco, and Paraguay, however, there are some rivers that don't have them. I wouldn't stick a toe in one just to find out if it did, though. The stories told in South America are horrible tales of people and animals accidentally falling into a stream from a boat or a slippery bank, and literally being eaten alive by these bloodthirsty little devils. I think I'd rather be a scout for General Custer.

Actually, the food they eat most is other fishes. But birds, reptiles, mammals, or any other hapless creatures that get into the water, either on purpose or accidentally, are usually bunches of bones in nothing flat. And strangely enough, they also eat fruit, which by this time is as startling as telling you that pork comes from a pig.

The piranha has a bulldog-like profile, with the lower jaw projecting out beyond the upper part of the face. He's a kind of silvery blue in color, with the lower rear fin a sort of reddish-orange hue, and he darts hither and yon with a speed that's hard to believe. It might not suit your taste, but a solitary piranha makes a fine pet, providing you don't want to pat him on the head too often, and just think of the fun you can have by dropping him into your mother-in-law's bath on a dull Saturday night.

A STICKY CUSTOMER

Crested Porcupine

As the baby porcupine said when he backed into a cactus, "Is that you, Mama?"

There's the short-tailed porcupine, the long-tailed porcupine, the brush-tailed porcupine, the North American tree porcupine, the prehensile-tailed porcupine, and the thin-spined porcupine, and they're all relative midgets when it comes to the biggest porcupine on earth, the crested porcupine. This sixty pound, over three foot long pin-cushion-with-legs, is found over most of Africa, all of southern Asia, throughout most of southeastern Europe, and in many zoos.

There are no bones in bananas, cats don't wear pajamas, you can't swim in a poolroom, and porcupines don't shoot their quills, but they're mighty good weapons anyhow. If you should annoy a porcupine, you'll know it, because he'll start wagging his tail, not in joy, but in warning, and when he does, the quills rattle a signal that sounds something like a rattlesnake's rattle. Then if friend porcupine is still being bothered, he'll turn his back and charge backwards with quills erect and usually succeed in planting a number of these needlepointed spines in tender flesh and nosy noses. The pest usually gets the point, or several of them.

The reason he's called the crested porcupine is actually because he has a crest, or mass of quills, stretching down his back from the nape of his neck to his short little cactus-like tail. If you take a close look at his quills, you'll find that they're long, tapered shafts with well polished surfaces that are ice-pick sharp at one end and attached loosely to the muscles just under the skin at the other end. Once they're stuck into the snout or the paws of an adversary, the quills easily leave the picky porc. And here's the sticker that makes the quill so dangerous. Along the shaft there are tiny, tiny barbs that lie flat until they're imbedded in someone's yielding flesh, and then they raise up and resemble miniature fishhooks that can't be removed without actually tearing out a little flesh right along with them. Sometimes the long bony weapons automatically work their way farther into the hapless victim, causing death to such losers as mountain lions, foxes, eagles, and even an occasional panther. And you thought a sliver was painful!

The crested porcupine makes his nest in a big, barren burrow. And he must like to dig, too, because oftimes the entrance to the burrow is a hundred feet from the bedroom, which makes it a long walk to answer the door. Apparently he doesn't like to live alone either, for many times there are as many as six or seven roommates sharing the burrow. He loves the bark of trees, sweet potatoes, pumpkins, or fallen fruit, and certainly doesn't endear himself to the farmer, for he chews the dickens out of farm crops with his sharp little teeth.

Usually two and sometimes three little ones are born at a time, coming into the world pretty well developed with their eyes wide open, and their little minds closed. They're not too bright as mammals go. Their spines, or quills, are pretty flexible, really on the soft side of things. The babies are left in the nest until their quills harden, about ten days, and then the little devils are really quite dangerous, just like a cantankerous mama or papa, although, as a general rule, porcupines aren't too aggressive.

The life expectancy of a crested porcupine is about twelve to fifteen years, but in zoos they've been known to bristle and bustle around for up to twenty years. And for those of you who've written to ask just how porcupines Indian wrestle, the answer is-----very cautiously, very cautiously!

PRANKSTER OF THE SEA

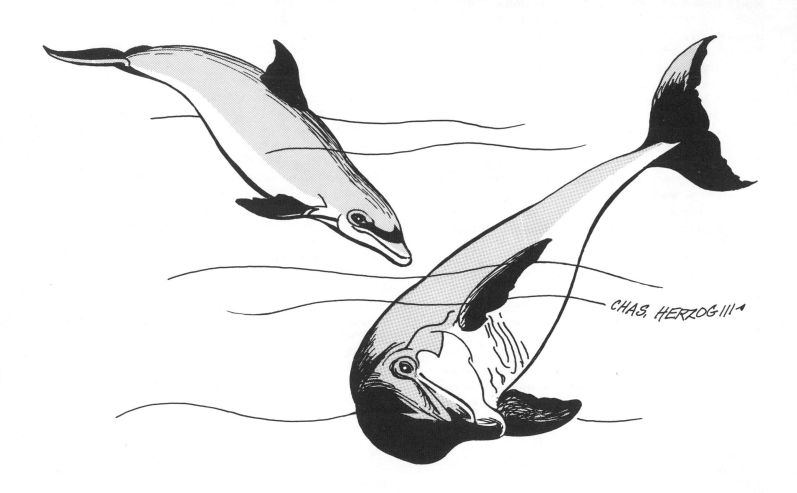

CHAS. HERZOG III

Porpoise

What's the difference between a single man and a married man? Easy----a single man has no buttons on his shirt. A married man----no shirt! Now, what's the difference between a dolphin and a porpoise? Just as easy. So far as can be told, the only difference is in the nose and head shape. The porpoise has a more blunt, rounded head, and no beak. The dolphin has a muzzle that's drawn out more in the shape of a beak----and of course, there are some in between shapes which could be classified under either name. You pays your money and you gets your choice. In any event, this aquatic mammal, this prankster of the sea, is intelligent and courageous and certainly couldn't be called the "chicken" of the sea.

There are more than twenty species of small whale, but it's easy to identify the porpoise. He has a gunmetal hide, usually ranges between eight and twelve feet long, and seems to have a built in smile, which is actually due to the natural curvature of his mouth. And he is friendly, with many stories told of porpoises saving human lives, of becoming playmates of children who live by the sea, of actually guiding ships through treacherous channels, like Flipper the Skipper, hurling his 300 pound body in reckless abandon and seeming glee as he races just ahead of the ship.

The peripatetic porpoise only has one nostril (would you call him a "half-breathe?"), and it's through this crescent-shaped blowhole that he makes his high squeaking voice, vibrating it like a human lip, making sounds like a berserk violinist in a G-string factory. He also breathes through this opening, which cleverly closes when it contacts the water. He can stay under water for over six minutes without coming up for air, for he is actually an air breathing mammal and not a fish at all.

And here's something that would drive mothers mad. He rarely sleeps from the time he's born until the time he goes to the final cradle of the deep thirty years later. Almost always in motion, he just dozes, partially submerged, in short intervals of thirty seconds to four minutes. And you thought you had insomnia! But the funniest story told of this delightful animal is the one about the nearsighted porpoise who fell in love with a small submarine, which isn't too funny until you consider the fact that everytime the submarine fired a torpedo---the porpoise handed out cigars!

DID YOU EVER SEE A BLOTTO POTTO?

Potto

I've heard of a hippo without a pottamus, and now and then I've heard of a hippie without a pot, but I've never heard of a potto that was ever "hip," because if the potto was "hip" he wouldn't spend his entire life in the trees, wouldn't travel upside down, and certainly wouldn't have his backbone partly outside his body!

Ah, the potto----a strange creature of the monkey world who looks like a little old man, with a big round face, large and limpid eyes, hands and feet out of proportion to his foot long body, and a head that hangs wearily in a down position, as though he were thinking that he'd bought a suit with two pair of pants and just burned a big hole in the jacket----or what's it all about, Herman?

Among mammals he is indeed unique, since no other mammal has his skeleton, or rather part of his skeleton sticking out, naked and unadorned. You see, the sharp little bones of his vertebrae actually are not covered with skin, and all along the back of the pooped out potto, they form a sharp ridge of bone tips about an eighth of an inch long that seemingly have no more use than feathers on a pump handle.

The exposed backbone, however, does have a use for the potto. He uses it like a concealed weapon, sort of a fur-covered switchblade. When danger comes, he stands up on his hind legs, as perky as you please, clenches his fists, and then suddenly does a kind of somersault into his unsuspecting adversary, which is something like hiding a horseshoe in your boxing glove. The sharp little spikes rip into the dum-dum who attacked in the first place and from that point on it's Band-aid time---or where did Mack the Knife come from?

The West African natives say that once the potto grabs and holds a branch with his powerful hands and feet, it's almost impossible to break his grip, even in death. Sometimes he travels upside down like the sloth, leisurely and lethargically, keeping a solid grip at all times, never letting go with one hand until he has a firm hold with the other. He hangs on as stubbornly as a tooth with ten roots.

The poor little potto, with soft, grizzled brown fur on his sides, and honey-yellow fur along his back, which he can raise or lower when he wants exposing his "weapon" or concealing it at will, has no set home or nest. He just lives all his life in the forest, rarely, if ever, coming to the ground. He wouldn't be a good ad for a mattress either. He sleeps during the day curled up in a ball, hanging to a branch of a tree hidden amongst the leaves. He eats leaves, fruit, and an occasional insect, has never been known to lead a protest march or drink to excess; after all how would it look to see a potto----blotto?

CHAS. HERZOG III

Bunny Rabbit

Once a year a furry, friendly, cuddly, quick, and gentle little creature takes credit for what the hens do all year long. Who in the western world hasn't heard of the Easter bunny and those wildly colored eggs that, rolled on a lawn, hidden under a couch, discovered in a corner, and put into baskets, turn green after a week on display, and then add a little sprightliness to dad's lunchbucket for another week? How come the bunny steps out of character and lays a little hen fruit on us for the Easter holiday?

Well, the whole, happy legend started hundreds of years ago, back when the Big Dipper was just a drinking cup and King Solomon only had sixty-nine wives. There was this Teutonic pixie, by the name of Ostara, so the story goes, who happened upon a bedraggled bird that was having trouble getting off the ground, and so Ostara, who also happened to be the Teutonic Goddess of Spring, just made a few secret, sorceress-like waves of her magic digits, and LO! the bedraggled bird instantly became a hippity-hoppity rabbit. The rabbit was so grateful for his new form that he promised thereafter to lay eggs every April when the festival of Ostara was celebrated, to sort of rejoice that winter was ended and spring was returning. See? Incidentally, our word *Easter* comes from the name of this pagan Goddess of Spring, Ostara.

Rabbits and hares are proverbially known as harmless and peace-loving creatures and that seems to be true, although they do have strong, hardy, rodent-like teeth that could put quite a dent on whatever they'd like to chomp on. However, they rarely bite humans, and their dispositions are as mild as well buttered artichokes, which accounts for their popularity as pets.

Of course, none of us like to split hares, but there is a difference between rabbits and hares and the difference is hardly worth mentioning. They both have small tails, large ears, long hind legs, thick, soft fur, and a million brave hunters killing them. But the major difference seems to be that a rabbit's babies are born blind and naked, while the hare's young are born with pretty good vision and a nice coat of fur. See, I told you it was hardly worth mentioning. In any event, in the United States hardly anyone makes the distinction between the two and they're usually all called rabbits, although hares are really larger.

And for folks who love large families, this charming little animal is just ideal. Generally speaking, rabbits give birth to litters of five or six as many as five times a year. Addition they don't know, but multiplying comes naturally. For instance, way back in the year 1859 there were only twenty-four rabbits in Australia, now there are millions. They multiplied so rapidly that they threatened to nibble the Australian plains bare, and so, foxes were brought in to keep the rabbit population down and control their numbers. It didn't work out too well, and today Australia has two problems, rabbits AND foxes.

Even though they are sometimes harmful to crops and stuff-like-that-there, they do a good job of supplying man with food and clothing. Rabbit skins make fine fur coats. Most of the felt used in hats comes from rabbit fur, their flesh is usually quite palatable, and, of course, Angora wool from the Angora rabbit not only clings to a man's suit, but makes a warm fluffy sweater besides. And, I'm told that bunnies make good waitresses too. Playboy bunnies, that is. So you see, the rabbit is beneficial to man and child. It just depends on your age as to which benefit you enjoy most.

ROCKY RACCOON IS A SMARTY

Raccoon

Quickly now, what do the giant panda, the cacomistle, the coatimundi and the kinkajou, have in common? If you answered that they're all relatives, you're absolutely right. However, if you don't include the neat and intelligent raccoon among them, then you'll have trouble with the naturalists, who claim that they all have so many similar characteristics that they must be in the same family. They are, and the family name is *Procyonidae*, which would be an easy name for any play-by-play announcer to mangle.

In some families, every day is Halloween, and with the raccoon clan, they wear their masks not only on Halloween, but every day as well, mostly because they're born with those "burglar" masks that help identify them as raccoons. They also have the usual rings on their tails, and nothing on their fingers. And while their tails can be a fluffy ten inches long, their fingers are bare-skinned and delicate and sensitive and seem to give them a dainty and finicky manner when they eat. And they'll eat most anything.

The roly-poly raccoon can snag a bird, gulp an egg, nibble on nuts, and use fruits and berries for desert. Since he can swim like a lifeguard in Venice, he's also able to catch fish, frogs, salamanders, and crayfish, and when the corn is on the cob he makes a pretty good pest of himself in some poor farmer's field. With a diet like that no wonder he's on the fat side of things! There are records of raccoons getting up to fifty pounds, but fifteen pounds is more the average, and people who hunt raccoons for food, say they taste like fat wombat. There's no accounting for taste, is there?

Many think that the little masked marvel is the cleanest creature in the wild because of his strange habit of washing or soaking his food in water before he eats it. Nobody really knows why he does it, not even the raccoon. No matter how clean the food is, he'll wash it. It seems to be just one of those natural nervous habits, like the dog turning around before he lies down. If no water is available he'll eat the food anyhow—but it makes him cranky.

The common housefly thinks humans are silly because they make such nice clean ceilings, and then walk on the floor. The raccoon is much the same. He's got such nice trees, and he can climb almost as well as a monkey, but he spends most of his waking time on the ground and only seems to take to the trees when his life is threatened. And just like the bears, after a busy summer of resting by day and prowling by night, he finds a nice, dark den to hole up in and then just hibernates till spring, which isn't a bad idea after realizing what kind of shape the world is in.

Way back when Davy Crockett was king of the wild frontier, and a bug was a tiny insect and not a device for eavesdropping, the raccoon was hunted not only for meat, but for the wherewithal with which to make a hat. Tail and all. And in the twenties, raccoon coats were all the rage. Even today the poor little raccoon is popular with the fur trade, only now they give it a more attractive name, like "Alaska sable." You just can't trust nobody, no more.

A TOTAL TEETOTALER

CHAS. HERZOG III

Kangaroo Rat

The late Humphrey Bogart once said that he didn't trust a camel or any other animal that didn't take a drink once in a while. He'd have hated the kangaroo rat-----he never drinks from the time he leaves the warmth of mama's breast to the time he stops breathing two to three years later.

This jumpy little animal lives in the warm, dry parts of western North America, from way down Mexico way up into Oregon, and even if he had a chance to drink he wouldn't take it because he gets all the necessary moisture from small, juicy little underground tubers that are usually found an inch or two below the surface of the ground, an insult to a good drink, but he just swallows the insult, and goes right on chomping.

This charming little rodent, when mature, is about twelve inches long, but seven inches of this length is tail, which is a whale of a tail with a bushy tip, but it's most important because, as he jumps around, the tail acts as sort of a ballast, giving him balance while he's in the air. And he's in the air a good deal of the time, being both nervous in nature and jumpy by design. The kangaroo rat can jump six to eight feet per leap, using his strong hind legs much the same as a kangaroo, and now you know how he comes by his name.

He's kind of handsome in a rodent-like way with a large oval head, small ears, and great big round dark eyes, the better to see with as he hops and jumps around mostly during the nighttime hours. Behind each tiny ear is a large patch of white fur, and a long racing stripe of white fur stretches from his hips to his tail, while his entire underside is a snowy white. The rest of him is a pleasant soft tan or gray, and he has dirty fingernails 'cause he likes to burrow in the sand.

He collects seeds mostly from a variety of plants and, quicker than you can say "Dipodomys Cratogeomys," he pops them into little pouches or pockets on either side of his mouth, using his short forefeet. Then when he returns to the underground burrow he calls home, he shoots the seeds out like you and I would squirt out watermelon seeds, using his forefeet once again to help squeeze them out. They say that it's not unusual for the kangaroo rat to collect and store as much as fifty quarts of seeds in his food locker, and he couldn't care less about the problem of inflation.

Most of the time this seedy little character lives as alone as Adam in Eden, although during the breeding season he gets pretty chummy, as you might suspect. However, all other times he seems to have the disposition of a cannibal during the fruit and berry season, and if you put two of them together they'll usually fight to the death. Strangely enough, they don't use their teeth in battle, they leap, bob and weave, and claw with their strong hind feet, making no vocal sounds, just battling until one has gone the way of all inside straights, and the other walking off with all the marbles. Which proves once again that the only place in the world that all nations can stick together—is in a stamp album!

RUDOLPH AND HIS COUSINS

Reindeer

Ah, Christmas time, the time of the year when that jolly little red-cheeked elf comes in through a hole in your roof and leaves through a hole in your pocket; a time when the only difference between men and boys is the cost of their toys; a time when Rudolph, the red-nosed hat rack with legs, leads the other members of his team on their happy yearly flight. And just what kind of animal is Rudolph? Why, a reindeer, of course, unless he's not domesticated, in which case he's called a *caribou.*

Reindeer have been called "camels of the frozen north," ranging way beyond the timberline into the Arctic Circle. They're the only deer in which both sexes have antlers; even the little fawns grow small spikes within two months of birth—and they know how to use them too. They're not always the friendly, soft-eyed, warm hearted beasts that wait patiently on the roof for dear old Santa. During the mating season, when they're in a fighting mood, they can be mighty dangerous, filling the Arctic air with the crack of their antlers as the bulls fight to be sultan of the harem.

Travel agencies would make a good buck (no pun intended) if they booked the reindeer, because of all the deer, this is the most migratory one. Thousands of them collect in August in one great herd and move out of the tundra regions, down to the shelter of the timber, hundreds of miles to the south. And when they're all gracefully trotting along they make a noise like a million electric typewriters working overtime, producing a distinct clicking sound. The noise isn't made by the wide, wide hooves clacking, but rather by the ankle joints clicking. Honest.

Now and then the reindeer might run into a grizzly, a wolverine, or a lynx, but, as a general rule, he has no real enemies on the Arctic tundra, although keeping a wolf away from his door can be quite a problem, the great Arctic white wolf, that is. But in an open chase the reindeer will outrun the wolf, running in a fast-swinging trot that he can keep up almost indefinitely. And he's a heck of a good swimmer too.

Strangely, the worst enemies of the reindeer are the mosquito and the botfly. The mosquitoes form a great and dense cloud around him, biting like a bedbug with buck teeth, making the poor animal keep constantly on the move, always headed into the wind, always looking for a high, windswept ridge or a snow-filled gulley to escape their attack, while the botfly is even more uncomfortable as it burrows into his hide to lay its eggs. It's enough to drive a harried reindeer to the nearest psychiatrist.

It used to be said that the chicken was the most useful animal in the world, because it could be eaten before it was born and after it was dead, but after checking out the reindeer I'm not so sure. For instance, the northern Indian and Eskimo use every conceivable part of this handy beast. They use the blood for soup, the flesh for steaks, the bones are crushed for marrow, the shin bone for knives, the horns for fishhooks, the tendons for thread, the skin for clothing, the hair for stuffing mattresses, the stomach membranes for big "baggies," even the partially digested food found in the stomach is eaten! And the reindeer milk, which is four times as rich in butterfat as cow's milk, is made into cheese. And when old St. Nick gets into the act as a teamster . . . well, it sort of makes you feel inadequate, doesn't it?

DON'T LAUGH AT POINTY TOUPEES

Rhinocerous

He's big, thick skinned, short legged, nearsighted, big headed, rushes headlong at great speed without thinking, and is capable of doing great damage. And if that description doesn't fit an irresponsible politician, then my name isn't *Rhinocerotidae,* and it isn't, but it is the name of an animal that is much maligned and too fast becoming extinct.

The ungainly creature with the short temper and the long horns is a somewhat tempermental behemoth called the *African black rhinocerous,* a beast which if left alone leaves everybody else alone. He wants no trouble, gives no trouble, usually has no trouble, just browses about looking for foliage, grasses, twigs, leaves (he's a strict vegetarian, y'know), wallows in mud, bathes in the dust, and takes an occasional swim. Doesn't sound so ferocious, does he?

A full-grown male can weigh up to 3,200 pounds, stand 5 feet tall at the shoulder, and charge viciously straight ahead at speeds up to 35 miles an hour. What makes him charge? Nobody really seems to know. He hears well, has a good sense of smell, but his eyes are not too strong, and, if the truth be known . . . he's just not too bright an animal.

The rhinocerous has a big head, which doesn't mean he's egotistical, it just means he has a big head with one of the most interesting weapons in the animal kingdom, the horn, or in the case of the African black, or hook-lipped rhino, two horns. You'd think that the horn would be solid bone to do as much damage as it can do, but that isn't true. The horn is actually an outgrowth of skin and made of a tremendous consolidation of hair. Sort of a pointy toupee. Sometimes the horns on a female are longer than the male's, and generally the front horn is a couple of inches longer than the rear one, with the record being fifty-four inches. However, the average length is about twenty-seven inches, just the right length for going to masquerade parties disguised as a unicorn.

His upper lip looks like an elephant's lower lip, although he's not related. It comes to a point and he can use it like a grasping finger to snatch shoots, leaves, and twigs, and draw them into his mouth. He's not too friendly even with other rhinos, and finding more than two of these beasts together is as surprising as hearing a goldfish sing. His tough hide is one half to three quarters of an inch thick, and in the old days made great fighting shields for the natives. And I'm told that the flesh of a rhino is just as tough as his skin, and that you had to pound it with a rock until it become palatable enough to eat, just like my butcher does. However, the liver is considered a great delicacy in hard-chewing parts of Africa.

The reason that he loves to wallow in the dust and wet mud, is mainly to rid himself of ticks and wee beasties that bite and bug, and to help in this chore there are strange little friends called *tick-birds* that dart and dance about the rhino's head and back, feasting on these little insect pests.

As large as the rhino is, as armorplated as he is, as well armed as he is, you'd think he's be afraid of no animal. And he's not, although there is one exception. The one creature that the rhino always is courteous to, always gives the right of way to, is the largest land animal in the world, the elephant. And who can blame him? The only record of an encounter between an elephant and a rhino was way back in the year 1500, when King Manuel of Portugal staged the fight. The rhino charged, the elephant grabbed with his trunk, the rhino flipped, and the elephant used his tusks to make shish kebab. No contest, no fight, no rhino!

SWORDSMAN OF THE SEA

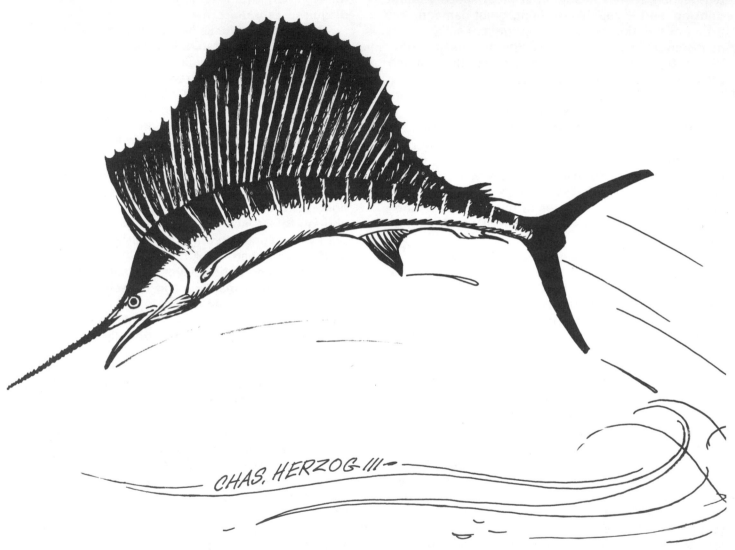

Sailfish

The fisherman's dream is to find a spot where the fish are so anxious that you have to hide behind a tree to bait the hook. Another dream of fishermen is to hook a fighting marlin or a soaring sailfish, both wonderful game fishes that live in the Atlantic and the Pacific. Powerful, streamlined creatures that delight the eye and quicken the pulse. The sailfish looks like a marine torpedo as it slices through the water at speeds up to sixty miles an hour, but only in short bursts. You'd think that the tremendous dorsal fin, that gives this interesting animal its name, would get in the way when swimming at a rapid rate, but old Mama Nature has solved the problem in a nice, easy, commonsense kind of way. The great fin just folds down into a most convenient groove in the back, much the same as a windshield wiper on a modern car disappears. Groovy! No one's really sure just what good such a large sailfin is anyway, though it might come in handy when some freeloader down on his luck asks if you can spare a "fin." Yuk, yuk.

The back of a sailfish is a rich, dark blue, and the underside light colored, which adds to the illusion of a torpedo when it streaks through the sea. The ones found in the Pacific are somewhat larger than the ones found in the Atlantic. Maybe the fish and the squid in the Pacific have more protein than in the Atlantic. In any event, the Pacific sailfish have been weighed in at close to 190 pounds while the record catch in the Atlantic only tipped the scales at 123 pounds, and that's a heck of a lot of fish to catch with a rod and reel.

When this beautiful creature is just a little swimmer, his jaws are about equal in length. He even has teeth. Then, as he grows, his jaws enlarge, but the teeth disappear, and the sailfin begins to blossom. By the time he's mature, the upper jaw has far outdistanced the lower jaw and becomes the spear that helps him win his food. However, the bulk of his meals are caught just because he has great speed and maneuverability; although there are stories of the sailfish impaling his prey on his sharp pointed weapon. Sort of like a D'Artagnan of the deep.

The relatives of the sailfish are much larger. The record marlin, for instance, weighed in at over 1,200 pounds, but he was caught in a net by Cuban fishermen and hijacked to Florida for pictures. The largest marlin ever caught by rod and reel was a 742 pound giant and measured 12 feet 11 inches. Even larger is the real swordsman of the sea, the broadbilled swordfish, who not only uses his sword in fighting, but does most of his hunting by roaring into a school of herring or mackerel, slashing both right and left, to say nothing of to and fro, maiming the hapless prey, which he then proceeds to gulp and gobble in his own sweet, unhurried way. And he's never been heard to mutter "En Garde" either!

Scorpion

I read recently of the Agriculture Department's great new idea for increasing egg production by having farmers hang pictures of Colonel Sanders in the hen houses! Then I read about some dude who swore that if you poured a circle of gasoline on the sand around a scorpion, and set the ring on fire, he would commit suicide by stinging himself to death rather than face capture or burning. Both stories are as phony as a marble toupee.

Once you see one scorpion, you've seen them all, in a manner of speaking, because all scorpions are basically alike. There are about 400 kinds of these crawly invertebrates scooting around in most warm, dry countries on the globe, and they all have eight legs, and an abdomen that ends in a sort of segmented tail that curves gracefully over his back and waves in all directions like a publicity-conscious actress at a cocktail party. At the end of this tail is a stinger loaded with enough poison to knock off the insects he eats. You might say he had a little zing in his sting.

These creepy, scuttling little devils range in size from eight inches long, like the shiny, black ones found in profusion in tropical jungles, down to the thin, pale creatures that live in the sandy wastes and are mature at about one inch long. If you're just a little curious and want to see one of the thirty-five species that live in the United States, the west and southwest desert regions are your best bet. Or maybe you'd rather go to Mexico, southern Europe, or northern Africa, where they're as commonplace as cornstalks in Kansas.

Unless you really hunt for this scurrying little horror, you'd have a tough time seeing one, because it's a nighttime creature coming out only when it's dark to hunt spiders and other insects—they don't particularly like heat or light. During the day they spend their time in their dens, working up an appetite. Sort of like show-biz folks. And what a den—just a hollowed out place under a stone, a log, in the sand, behind some loose bark, or any other piece of flotsam or jetsam they might find unoccupied by another scorpion or bug. But be careful if you find one!

His sting will cause a pretty painful wound and scare you half to death. He has enough poison to kill a small meal on the hoof, but he really doesn't have enough to seriously harm a human. At least there's no record of one ever having killed a full grown man. But then, they don't seem to keep records of half-grown men. Leave them alone, even if you were born under the sign of Scorpio.

Not only do they have that stinger, but they also have two great big, lobster-like pinchers with the strange name of *pedipalpi*, which grab, hold, and squeeze their prey. They don't lay eggs, either, but give birth to living young, who, as soon as they're born, climb up on Mama's Scorpion's back and ride around until mama molts, and then they hop off and fend for themselves. All the while they're up there they eat a big fat nothing, living off the stored up energy of their own bodies, and that gave rise to another old wives' tale that says they eat the body of their mother. Nonsense, mama's back is hard and babies' jaws are weak, so get off my back.

THE ANSWER TO WOMEN'S LIB

Seahorse

Once upon a long time ago, a most delightful nephew drew himself up to his full three foot height and queried a query designed for whimsy. "What," he squeaked, "is red, has feathers, and goes bah, bah, bah?" I shook my head. "The thing that is red, has feathers, and goes bah, bah,bah-----is an Indian singing the 'Whiffenpoof Song!'"

Not bad—but how about this one? What has the head like that of a horse, an external skeleton like that of an insect, a grasping tail like that of a monkey, eyes that can be moved independently like those of a chameleon, and a pouch for carrying its offspring like that of a kangaroo? This is a pretty wild assortment, and I wouldn't blame you if you said that there is no such animal. Ah, but there is! And we call it the *seahorse!*

What a pity that these interesting fish, for fish they are, are so finicky about their food, and so dependent on sea water—otherwise they'd make the craziest pets. Gentle, quiet, undemanding, and they can't turn on you. If they do, just take the salt out of their water, which would take the pep out of their step, the zest out of their vest. It would also kill them.

There are about fifty different species of seahorses and while they're usually found in shallow water, some have been found floating in seaweed many, many miles from land, but always in tropical or temperate seas. Of the fifty different kinds, the largest known is the western Atlantic that lives offshore, from southern California down to northern Peru, and gets about one foot in length, while the smallest is between one and two inches long, and describes the kind of horse I usually bet on. You should see the jockey!

Actually, they look like dignified chess pieces, a unique knight of the first water. The whole body is encased in jointed armor, really an external skeleton that they have in addition to the more conventional internal skeleton of all backboned animals. And the mouth is also most interesting. It's small and traplike, and located right at the tip of a long snout, but it seems just perfect for snapping up even smaller crustaceans, which slide into the toothless jaws and are swallowed whole.

About half of a seahorse is tail, which is flexible and prehensile or grasping, and since it's not one of the brightest or most mobile of fishes, it spends a good deal of its time just a-grabbing and a-holding to undersea objects as it makes its slower than slow progress from place to place . . . about as fast as a snockered snail. Just how does this unique fish move about, anyhow? Well, next time you get a chance, look closely at the small, transparent fins on the chest and back of this sodden, upright refugee from a surrealist sea. These fins may be hard to notice moving, but move they do, vibrating back and forth as fast as thirty-five times a second, giving the fishy horse a deliberate and dignified forward motion, as though he were riding a bicycle that wasn't there.

However, the dignity of the male seems to fade and the female's cleverness really begins to show, because the female seahorse realizes the dream of every mother since the beginning of time—she lets the old man have the babies! It's poppa who actually carries and nurtures the young until birth. Mama Seahorse deposits the eggs into a special pouch that the male seahorse has on his belly. The pouch is then sealed and fertilization takes place. And then, in the Atlantic seahorse, about 45 days later, 150 to 200 baby seahorses gallop out. I wonder if any of daddy's funny finny friends hang around and shout, "They're off!"

LIVING IS EASY
FOR FATTY SEAL

CHAS. HERZOG III.

Elephant Seal

He's big, he's ugly, he's clumsy, and he's becoming extinct. He's also the largest seal in sealdom, which is why he's called the *elephant seal,* sometimes weighing well over 5,000 pounds. He rarely gets ruffled, seems to have no temper, and if someone should inadvertently disturb his beachside slumber, all he does is flick his powerful front flipper, a shower of sand and stones is directed at the intruder, and then, before you can say the latin word *mirounga,* he's back to sleep again.

Only three things concern this giant among seals. One: food. Two: sleep. Three: lady seals. In that order. Nothing else seems to ever concern this large, hungry, sleepy, sexy mammal. When he eats, he dives deep, deep, down in the sea, seeking small sharks, squiggly squids, and fish that swim slower than he does . . . and he swims at a pretty good clip too. He may be clumsy on land, but in the water, he's as graceful as a swan with two necks.

Seals don't have teeth designed for crushing or grinding food, they just have sharp, pointed teeth that are ideal for grabbing and holding, and so they swallow their food whole and alive. They don't chew, and as everyone knows, that can lead to a need for a lifetime supply of Alka-Seltzer. And so to help grind up their food, they swallow stones and gravel and not just a little bit either, but as much as twenty pounds with some of the stones as large as hen's eggs. That's getting stoned the hard way.

The wise ones who name animals called this the *elephant seal* not only for his great size, but also for a strange looking trunk-like bag, snout, or schnozzle that has about as much use as a tire pump in a canoe. This blubbery bag hangs like a limp balloon about eight or nine inches below the seal's mouth, and when he fills his lungs with air and lets out his characteristic bellow, the trunk-like thing swells with air, the tip curls into his mouth, and the roar is something like an anguished bagpipe that's just backed into a frigid air conditioner. If the darn thing ever backfired he could blow his tonsils through the back of his fat head.

He's fat. You don't weigh over 5,000 pounds and not be fat. An unusually thick layer of fat just underneath his hide makes him actually quiver like a tremendous bowl of Jello when he lumbers along on land, which is quite a sight when you consider that the male elephant seal reaches a length of twenty feet. Females only quiver half as much, because they're only ten feet long on the average.

They used to hunt this hapless creature with great intensity because his fat and his oil were so profitable. But today the herds are so small, the seals so scarce, that it hardly pays to hunt them, I'm glad to say. They come ashore about the middle of August, wait for the unwary females to follow, then pick the ladies of their choice to stock their harems, brawl and breed, then breed some more, and in a month or so they're back just eating and sleeping again. Ah, sweet mystery of life------maybe they've solved it.

Sheep

It's mighty difficult to tell the Alka from the Seltzer, it's sometimes a chore to tell the Procter from the Gamble, but if you really want a problem, try and tell the sheep from the goats. You'd think it'd be an easy job, but really it isn't, mostly because there are many similarities. For instance, both animals' ancestors lived in the mountains; both chew cuds, and both have hollow horns and hairy (sometimes wooly) coats. However, there are differences such as the horns of a goat grow upward and backward, while a sheep's are spirally curved. Male goats have beards, are more sure-footed than their cousins, and have a distinct characteristic that immediately makes you think somebody forgot the Right Guard. And, of course, grownup goats are generally pugnacious; and sheep, peaceful.

The sheep was an important animal in biblical times, even more than today, and no animal gets more mention in the Bible than the domestic sheep. Of course, there are great differences between the wild sheep and the domestic variety, with the most notable being the long tail and wooly fleece on the tame type. The wild members of the family have short tails and stiff, hairy coats, and only the careful and stubborn work of man is responsible for the wooly sheep as we know it today. He crossbred and crossbred until he came up with just what he wanted. Apparently, what he wanted was a sheep that had soft wool that could be woven and mutton that could be palatable. As a result there are now forty breeds of domestic sheep, and I still don't like the way they taste.

Australia, Western Asia, the western parts of the United States and Britain are mainly responsible for most of the world's wool, while the Merino sheep of Spain is said to have the finest wool in the world. In the semi-arid regions of the Soviet Union there's a poor little lamb that gives up his pelt between the age of one week and ten days to make the coat called the Persian lamb or caracul or broadtail. Bah, bah, black sheep, I say.

There are tribes in Asia that live almost exclusively on mutton, and so they've developed a breed most aptly suited to their needs. It's called the *dumba* and is sometimes referred to as the sheep with the forty pound tail because it's excessively fat in the buttocks and can actually have a long, fat tail that weighs forty pounds. There are even stories of prize-winning specimens that have to carry their tails in little carts behind them, which is a far cry from pulling the wool over their eyes. The wool of the dumba is used for clothing too, and some of the tribesmen beat it into a resilient felt and cover their tents with it, which makes this a pretty useful animal. You can eat it, wear it, and live in it.

In ancient times sheep were kept more for milk than meat, while just the opposite seems to be true today. When was the last time you heard someone ask for a glass of sheep's milk? It's as rare as a campaign button in a nudist camp, although the French discovered that sheep's milk made wonderful cheese, and still does . . . it's called *roquefort*.

A GREEDY
LITTLE ASSASSIN

CHAS. HERZOG III

Shrew

The question as to which is the most ferocious animal in the world immediately makes you think of lions, tigers, cobras, grizzlies, and the like, and then when you find the answer it's as surprising as hearing a goldfish sing "O Sole Mio." The answer is . . . the shrew.

A bloodthirsty, savage, and fierce little beast that knows no fear, is so wild a fighter that he'll attack, kill, and eat animals twice his size, can eat the equivalent of his own weight every three hours, and uses up energy so quickly that if deprived of food he'll starve to death in less than one day! It's sort of comforting to know that he's such a tiny animal, weighing about two to the ounce. If nature had made him a little bigger maybe he'd be writing this article about us.

You may have already seen a shrew and mistaken him for a mouse, just a furry, grey, velvety blur with a sharp little muzzle and barely visible pinhead eyes, hurrying and scurrying nervously through the grass, sniffing out his prey, finding a beetle, cricket, slug, or centipede and springing like the deadly killer he is, slashing and slaying. He'll eat almost anything he can kill, and so quickly that he shakes and shivers in excitement as he gobbles.

Nonetheless, be not too dismayed at this viciousness, m' hearties . . . there's some good in everything! Even a weather forecast is right now and then, and this greedy little assassin maintains a nice balance in nature by doing away with hordes of injurious insects of all kinds, making the shrew a pretty valuable little creature in the great scheme of things. Shrews live just below the surface of the ground, and life usually begins for these little bloodthirsty midgets in a loose ball of leaves and grasses, hidden in a burrow of some other small animal, or a log, or a stump. Between four and ten are born at a time, pink and crinkly, about the size of honeybees. They creep and crawl in a week, are weaned on earthworms in three weeks, are booted out of the old homestead at four weeks, and are on their own until they die of old age . . . in about sixteen months.

This obnoxious little fighter has, as you might suspect, lots of enemies. Cats, foxes, owls, snakes, hawks, weasels, and even fish will kill a shrew on sight, but they won't eat him because, to put it bluntly, he smells. I guess he never heard of deodorants, and even if he had, it would soon wear off. A pair of glands, one on each flank, that secrete a miserable, musky odor, make only animals without a sense of smell able to stand the stench.

Most shrews have poisonous saliva glands in the lower jaw, something like the venom of a weak cobra, and while the poison has little or no effect on a human being, it is strong enough to fog the mind of his victim, with the bite of the short tailed shrew capable of killing a full grown mouse.

The thing that distinguishes the savage shrew from other animals is his front teeth. Those of the upper jaw are hooked and even have a little fishhook prong . . . the better to slash you with, my dear. The shrew is afraid of nothing. Naturalists tell of the shrew that was put in a cage with a medium-sized white rat. Instantly, the little fury reared up, bared his teeth, let loose a high-pitched staccato squeak, and in a flash was across the cage, slashing at the rat's throat, swarming all over him and in less time than it takes to get an eerie feeling, the rat was gone, including bones, claws, and fur.

It's even fatal putting two shrews in the same cage, because in just a few minutes there'll be just one, licking his chops and wondering where his next meal is coming from. I wonder why they call some women "shrews," and how you go about taming one?

CHARMING LITTLE STINKER

Skunk

There's a new deodorant on the market called Gone. Spray it on and YOU disappear; then everyone stands around and wonders where the odor is coming from! And that leads us into looking at a little animal, about the size of a house cat, that has absolutely no need of a deodorant—the king of defensive chemical warfare, the dangerous but not deadly—skunk.

This charming little stinker, believe it or not, carries two guns, and like the good guy in the Zane Grey western, won't use his weapons unless really provoked, frightened, or annoyed, but when he does---Look Out! He's deadly at nine feet and more, and a blast from close range not only blankets you with a stench that would make the kids tip you over on Halloween, but causes the tears to flow freely and can even cause temporary blindness.

He hates to waste ammunition, and uses his two guns, or glands, only as a last resort. The first barrage is most powerful, as you might suspect, and both guns can be fired separately or together, with enough ammo at the base of the tail for six consecutive shots. The Wyatt Earp of the mammalian world! Only worse, because with Wyatt you're dead—with a good blast from this striped pussycat, you'll wish you *were* dead.

The penetrating odor hangs on like a second coat of paint and it seems the only remedy is to have the garments cleaned and burned. Old skunky must realize how odiferous and miserable his oily, yellow weapon is, because he seems to be extremely careful not to get any of the evil smelling liquid on himself. The victim howls and the pussycat with the secret weapon ambles off as pure and fragrant as ever.

Strangely enough, the malodorous mess, the fluid produced by the skunk, can be refined, the disagreeable smell removed, and the residue blended with other alluring scents. The result: a fine perfume. I think it's called "Three Days on a Troop Train."

Anyhow, the four-legged aerosol bomb is a pretty hard customer to run into during the daylight hours because he's active mostly at night, and then he's sort of slow and deliberate in his actions as he scrounges for insects, the staple in his diet. Occasionally he'll speed up to a trot to catch an unwary mouse, snake, or frog, although any kind of creeping thing is food for a skunk. And since skunks are reasonably easy to capture, scent glands easy to remove, and diet easy to supply, the skunk makes an ideal pet, easy-going and loving.

Of course, the house will be free of rodents and any kind of creeping thing. The house may also be free of guests as well, if they're not told that your skunk isn't loaded. During the mating season two suitors may fight quite bitterly for the possession of a female . . . they may even forget to "fight fair" and spray each other with their own obnoxious liquid, which is a dirty trick even for a skunk, love and war notwithstanding. After all they do belong to the same union. Incidentally, the smell of the skunk may carry farther than a half mile.

The striped skunk is at home in Canada, the United States, and as far south as Honduras, and their pelts are in demand in the fur trade. They're sold under the pleasing names of "Alaska sable" or "black marten." Ah, yes, a skunk by any other name----is an interesting creature----but have you ever considered that maybe they don't like the way we smell either?

CHAS. HERZOG. III

Snail

Some smart scientist has finally come up with the something that will definitely kill crabgrass . . . it's called *winter.* But no one, it seems, since time began, has come up with a way to kill a snail. I don't mean one particular snail, but the family, the family of mollusks, animals with shells. Who would want to kill such an inoffensive little creature, anyhow? Unless you're French and love "escargots," in which case, count me in, with plenty of garlic butter.

We really don't know anything definite about the early, early ancestors of this slowpoke, except that as other life forms changed, added, multiplied, and evolved, the lowly snail just added a shell. He creeps slowly along through the ages eating little, and, as long as no danger threatens, he'll put his one foot out and move with all the speed of an atrophied ant in a deep freeze. Actually, if you use a stopwatch, you'll find that on a straightaway a snail will move at the astounding speed of three inches in one minute. He can make a yard in twelve minutes and a mile in fifteen *days,* which sounds like the kind of animals I bet on.

The average snail without the shell weighs around one and a quarter grams; his shell weighs close to two grams; and the little piece of shell that he uses when he withdraws into his "house" and slams the door weighs less than you can imagine. If a human being had the same arrangement, he'd be a 125 pound man with a 200 pound shed on his back and a front door that weighed a half pound, (which might be a handy way to live when the bill collectors came looking for you).

Once this little speed demon starts walking, he turns neither right nor left and seems to move at the same pace whether he's on glass, wood, paper, or stone, spreading a sort of thin mucous-like fluid out ahead of him, something like an ice skater making ice to skate on. The fluid is lubrication, a smoothing substance, and a security blanket all in one; besides, when he gets where he's going he's not covered with dust.

Snails are found everywhere, with the greatest number living in the ocean. Some live in fresh water, some live on land, some like to live in the mountains, and some of the more stupid ones even live in the polar regions. Some have flattened shells, most have conical or spiraled shells, and a few poorer relatives in the family don't even have a shell—they're called *slugs.* In the tropics the snails live well and seem to grow much larger, with one found in the Amazon region growing as large as five inches in length, which is almost as strange as finding a snail in the tail of a quail.

VENOM AND VINEGAR—
THE CORAL SNAKE

CHAS. HERZOG-III

Coral Snake

When a man says that there are only sixty-nine types of women, all this proves is that he has met only sixty-nine women. Ah, but when the people who know snakes best tell you that there are only two kinds of coral snakes in the United States and both are venomous enough to make you name the executor of your will, then you'd better believe them. The coral snake is the closest relative to the cobra in the western hemisphere, and unfortunately lives in parts of America where it's much too easy to confuse it with the "false coral snakes."

The "false coral snake," you see, has red bands with black borders, while the real thing has red bands with yellow borders. If you're color-blind, you're in big trouble. The bite of one is as harmless as a cactus needle in the finger, the bite of the other is nonhabit forming. Two of the venomous varieties live in the southern parts of the country. One, the Sonoran coral snake, cavorts in Arizona and New Mexico, and ranges down into northwestern Mexico; the other, the Eastern coral snake, lives in Florida, along the Gulf Coast, and slithers up into the Carolinas. They're not very aggressive reptiles, so if you leave them alone, they'll leave you alone, which is pretty good advice for society in general.

The Sonoran specie rarely gets over a foot and a half in length, while the eastern cousin grows up to around three feet in length; and both have one thing in common, they're cannibals. They eat other snakes. It seems no other snake in the world is immune to their poison. They simply bite another creepy, crawly creature with their needle-like fangs, slip them a short shot of venom, and *Voila!* a reptilian gourmet's delight. Sometimes just to relieve the monotony they'll vary the diet with a tasty lizard or two.

South of the border, Señor, down Mexico way, there are several more species of coral snakes, and in South America they say that there are some of these beautifully striped snakes that grow past the five foot mark, and while they're brightly marked and not very thick in the body, they're also difficult to find. The main reason for their wraith-like quality is the fact that all coral snakes are burrowers and rarely come to the surface, which is all right by me. I always say "neither a burrower nor a lender be" . . . what do you say?

Coral snakes do not give birth to living young. They lay two to four eggs, and whether you want to believe it or not, snakes do not swallow their young in times of danger to protect them. Truth of the matter is, the youngsters don't even remain with the parents, they wiggle off on their own, full of venom and vinegar, ready to face the cruel world almost immediately. Many parents would probably agree that this is a pretty good idea and should be put into practice at age fifteen-----better make that twelve.

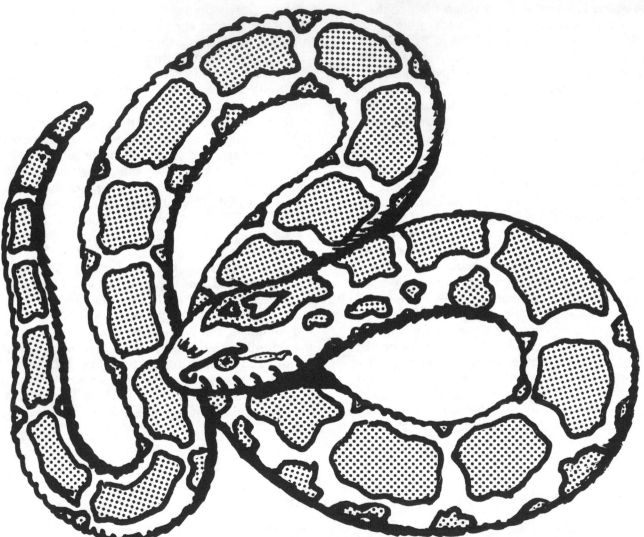

Milk Snake

There's a story around of the farmer who milked so many cows that he went around shaking hands one finger at a time . . . There's another story around of a snake called the *milk snake* that slithers into a barn, attaches itself firmly to the cow's milking apparatus and feeds to its heart's content, an experience that the cow finds so traumatic that she dries up and gives no milk for days afterward, which, of course, upsets the farmer who immediately dispatches the milk thief to that great snake pit in the sky. The only thing about both these stories is that they're both as phony as a pewter dime! . . . completely false.

Now, before everyone starts shouting that there is such a snake, a milk loving reptile, let me say that indeed, there is a snake here in the United States called a *milk snake,* but it has nothing to do with cows. True, the milk snake is found in barns, and is there for its meal, but it does not drink milk, and certainly not directly from the second faucet on the left. Rather, the milk snake is there to feed on delightful little mice and other snakes found around barns. The milk snake here in the United States is really a king snake and will occasionally even dine on a deadly rattler if it gets the opportunity.

To further squelch the thief-in-the-barn myth, the milk snake, like other snakes, has a real mouthful of teeth. These sharp little needles spring from both jaws as well as the roof of the mouth. It would have to be a very cooperative and masochistic cow to allow this toothy reptile to poach a little milk. Not only that, but the milk snake doesn't have the necessary digestive equipment to assimilate the food value in milk, even if you could find one that was hooked on this most unreptile-like diet.

The fable, both of stealing milk and liking milk, is a strangely prevalent one. For instance, in India the natives think the cobra is fond of milk, and if one of these deadly snakes is spotted in the backyard, the native will set out a bowl of milk for him, in hopes of pleasing him. In Mexico, the myth is even wilder. There they believe that the milk snake lurks in houses to steal the milk from expectant mothers! The whole thing is udderly ridiculous!

Rattlesnake

Instead of loving your enemies, treat your friends a little better! Ah, but what if you have no friends? Then, like the fellow who has limburger cheese in his moustache, the whole world smells! And it's a limburger world for the rattlesnake, for if ever there was a creature on earth without any friends, it's the cold-eyed terror, the rattlesnake.

The poor rattlesnake has to steal, slither, slip, and suffer from place to place, constantly on the defensive, always on the lookout for something to eat, or something to eat him. He knows that if it moves toward him, it's unfriendly. That could give you a real complex, Dr. Freud. The rattlesnake has a most disagreeable, uncertain life, unloved, misunderstood, and seemingly unwanted, as though he were the serpent who connived to get Adam and Eve out of Eden.

Human beings rarely miss an opportunity to club a rattler to death; other snakes kill and eat rattlers; hawks, owls, ravens, turkeys, and road runners knock off their share; even chickens eat baby rattlers just like they'd eat worms . . . Hogs aren't often affected by snakebite because their layers of fat don't absorb the poison, and so they enjoy a dietary tidbit of rattler; coyotes find them great fun to kill; ranchers destroy them to keep their livestock healthy; curators collect them for zoos and museums; and they even find their way into laboratories where the venom is squeezd out of them to make antidotes. And you think you have that hounded, harried feeling!! The most amazing thing is that rattlers survived at all.

The most universally recognized feature of this virile viper is the strange apparatus at the end of his tail, the rattle. Each time the snake sheds his skin (about three times a year on the average), a new segment, or rattle, is added to the string. Some of the rattles break off naturally, some are occasionally gnawed off by rats while the rattler is hibernating, and so it's almost impossible to determine the age of the reptile by the number of rattles. That's an old wives' tale, and so is the belief that a rattler can strike over half the length of his body, or will chase people, or that momma rattler will swallow her young to protect them, or that the rattler is a gentleman and will always rattle before striking . . . all baloney, no matter how thick you slice it.

There are at least twenty-eight kinds of rattlesnakes and they live in every state except Maine, Delaware, Alaska, and Hawaii, with the largest and most dangerous being the fat, eastern diamondback, found from the Carolinas down to Florida and over into Louisiana. They grow up to eight feet long and have a disposition like a grumpy grizzly with the gout. One of the smallest is the desert sidewinder, about two feet long, who finds that a sidewise slither is his shortest distance between two points. The Michigan rattler, the massasauga, is amongst the lesser of the poisonous evils, and there is no record of it ever killing a healthy adult. The record, however, has been known to be poorly kept on occasion.

Rattlesnakes eat rabbits, ground squirrels, gophers, rats, mice, birds, lizards, and they eat about once every two weeks. They have no table manners at all and are incapable of biting only a *piece* of something. They have to swallow it whole. And talk about heartburn! The gastric juices of a rattlesnake are so strong that even the teeth and bones swallowed are dissolved in just a few days! Bet he could take the serial numbers off the engine of a "hot" car just by breathing on them.

THE JET SET SQUID

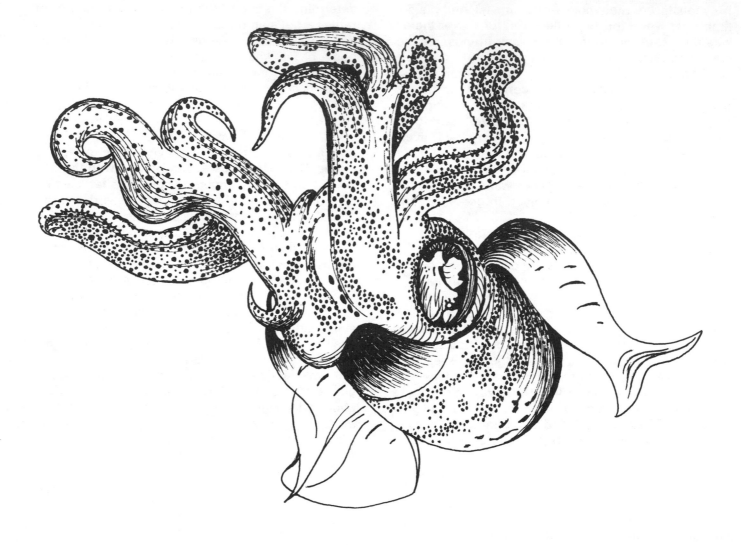

Squid

I don't know why, maybe it was those horror movies I enjoyed as a kid, but I always thought of a squid or an octopus as a man-eating creature that lurked in the dark depths of the sea, just waiting for a deep sea diver to float by so that he could zip out, wrap his eight legs around his hapless victim, the suction cups raising giant-sized hickeys, and drown and devour the poor, senseless human who was foolish enough to even come close.

Baloney, poppycock, and balderdash, to say nothing of malarkey! There's not much evidence to support those exciting tales that ancient authors and Hollywood moviemakers love to make into profitable adventures. Although, I suppose that an occasional octopus or giant squid could get large enough to give a man a hard time, it's more likely that some apocryphal and inventive scientist would cross an octopus with a bale of hay----and get a broom with eight handles.

The common squid is about eight inches long and built like a light-colored sausage, with a tapered tail that has two fins. Its diameter is roughly two inches and it darts through the water like a miniature torpedo. The head is flanked by two large eyes that not only look human, but upon examination, seem to be constructed pretty much the same way. The speed with which squid slash through the water in giant schools has earned them the nickname "sea arrows." Trying to catch one would be like trying to hold a handful of smoke on a windy day.

The sea arrow's body is sort of a dark gray with red spots, and when excited, especially during the mating season, he can flash a bright red, looking like a high-speed neon sign. They're caught in great quantities by use of nets and used primarily for bait in fishing for cod. The good folks who live along the Mediterranean and close to Oriental waters also find the common squid uncommonly good eating, especially the tentacles that wave and waver about six inches in front of the head and eyes. I'm not sure about you—but I have a little trouble eating eels too.

The common squid is a common sight along the Atlantic coast from Nova Scotia to Florida, while the giant squid is about as hard to find as a bashful Go-Go dancer. The giant squid lives in the open sea and few live ones have ever been seen. An occasional dead one may wash up on shore, especially around Newfoundland, but that's about all. The common squid, the giant squid, and the octopus all secrete an inky fluid which they use as a sort of smokescreen when some pests molest them, and they all have a method of getting around by sucking in water and then squirting it out an opening in a high speed hydraulic jet. You might even call them members of the sea-going "Jet Set."

THE STORK IS MOD

CHAS. HERZOG III

Stork

"Gee, grandma," asked the bright, bespectacled six year old, "Did the stork bring you?"

"Yes, Seymour, he did."

"And did he also bring daddy?" the precocious one pursued.

"He certainly did," chortled grandma.

"And how about me, did he bring me too?"

"Without a doubt, Seymour, the stork brought you too."

"Well, I'll be darned," said the young one, "You mean to tell me that there hasn't been any sex in our family for the past three generations!"

How does a legend get started, and why blame babies on the friendly old bird with the snow-white plumage and the long red legs? Apparently it's because of his long association with men. We have records of storks nesting on European roofs as long as 700 years ago with the story that the presence of a stork's nest on a roof not only protects the house from lightning, but that the lucky homeowner will live a long and healthy life and collect great wealth!

The original thought was that the stork who homesteaded on the roof was actually the soul of some departed ancestor, who took a lively interest in, and watched over the anticipated newcomer----sort of a friendly two-legged ghost.

The nest of the white stork isn't a sometime thing, either. It's a veritable birdland fort, castle, and sanctuary, used by succeeding generations of storks until, over a period of years, it can become a cylinder of interlaced twigs six feet high, four feet wide, so firmly anchored to a rooftop or chimney that even the strongest wind cannot make it shake, rattle, or roll. No need to worry about "Rock-A-Bye Baby" on the rooftop.

The stork in full bloom is about four feet high, with a white plump body, black wing feathers, a red bill, and long skinny legs that look as though you'd have to tie knots in them so that he'd have knees. The legs are in keeping with the modern trend, though, with red stockings for that sporty look. And strangely, the stork's vocal chords are useless, making nary a sound. They talk with their bills, however, by clapping the upper half against the lower half, making more noise than a cranky castanet gone kooky. Variations in tempo and volume make their emotions and meanings quite clear. He can rattle his bill like a machine gun when he's outraged, and be as quiet as two sweethearts in a hammock when he lays his bill along his mate's neck while wooing.

And storks really take care of their young, watching them closer than the ringmaster at a flea circus watches fleas. Ma and pa set a very nice table, complete with mice, moles, frogs, snails, small snakes, beetles, crickets, and grasshoppers, dropping these supersucculent tidbits into the center of the great nest and letting the youngsters pick at the smorgasbord for themselves. There's even a report that on hot, hot days an adult stork will bring water in his bill and let it trickle down into the bill of the parched babies . . . sort of a water bill.

Every year the European storks hit the road—and what a road! They make an annual 14,000 mile trip, winding up in South Africa where they spend the winter hunting on the grassland. Down there they're called "locust birds" because they gobble up locusts by the ton. Comes February, though, and the storks head back to the regions where they were born, many times right back to the identical neighborhood.

But alas and alack! Each year more and more nests are left empty, and mysteriously the storks of Europe are lessening and lessening. Now if only we could figure a way for babies to bring storks!

Swallow

One swallow doesn't make a summer, but too many swallows make a fall. And seventy-five kinds of swallows make up the family of birds that are the most graceful and delightful of the songbirds. They sweep and swerve, wheel and turn, swoop and swallow—swallow insects, that is, because that's why they sweep and swoop, to catch insects, which happens to be the only kind of food they eat.

All swallows have short, flat bills, but they can open those little bills so that they look like the gaping mouth of a change purse, the better to scoop the hapless bugs in, as they gracefully go about the business of being friendly and useful. Their legs are small and weak, and so are their feet, and as a result they do very little walking. Just perching mainly, but if you could fly like a swallow would you walk? No sir! Not even to the corner drugstore for a nice, fat fly.

Probably the best known of the swallow family is the barn swallow, a beautiful seven inch bird with a glistening black back, a reddish breast, and a long forked tail with white spots here and there. Way back in the days when children used to ask their parents where they came from instead of telling them where to go, barn swallows used to nest on cliffs, but now they nest on the beams of barns or ledges of buildings. One of the tamest of birds, he gobbles up scads of skittering, flittering insect pests, which makes him a good friend of man, who needs all the friends he can get nowadays.

Out in California, where Dean Martin's swimming pool measures 80 × 100 proof, there's a mission of San Capistrano, where a group of cliff swallows make their home. They build their nests in the form of large, round mudballs, with a spout for a door on the side. They line the nest with chicken feathers and lay four or five brown spotted eggs a season. It's easy to identify these swingers because they have a pretty good-sized orange spot on their lower backs. Anyhow, each winter the swallows hit the road on their migratory schedule and each spring they come back to Capistrano, from the song of the same name . . .

According to the legend, the wily birds set their internal watches at October 19 and take off to the south, then they set the clock for half-past March and arrive back on March 19. Not even leap year confuses them. However, some mean ornithologists, with no sense of what makes a good story for newspapers, say they're just not that accurate. However, most editors being the kind of people they are, keep right on using the story, adding to the legend. Maybe it's for the birds.

The largest swallow in America is an old friend called the *purple martin*, mostly because he's a dark blue—a dark, purplish blue, but blue nonetheless, which, if you stretch a color, is purple. The martins live in great groups, fat and sassy, singing up a storm and being pleasant. If you should have a flock living in one of your big birdhouses, keep an eye out for the pesky little English sparrows, because they'll push the martins out and move in, and not even sign a lease.

As for the old wive's tale that swallows hibernate in a hollow tree or in the mud at the bottom of a pond, forget it. They're just hard to find in the winter because they migrate, sometimes as much as 14,000 miles on their yearly round trip. Hard to believe? You could look it up—just a check with the famed Birdman of Lafayette Street, William Q. Lutz, a man who does an imitation of a bird so realistically, you're afraid to look up!

MARRIAGE IS FOREVER

Swan

196

It takes two to make a marriage----a single girl and an anxious mother! Among humans the marriage is for better or for worse, but not necessarily for good. Among swans it's definitely for life. When two of these long-necked, graceful birds get together and decide that love has found a way, they stay married and together to a ripe old age. Some experts say that a swan's ripe old age is about 100 years, other say 50 years, but a more reasonable estimate would be about 35 years; at least that's what the folks who keep swans in zoos and parks say, and who's to argue with an ornery ornithologist?

The legends surrounding the swans go all the way back to ancient times with the most famous, I think, the Greek myth of a goddess named Leda who had a swinging fling with a god who really was a wolf in swan's clothing. Anyhow, the Greeks called this big bird with the graceful movements and exquisite white plumage the "Bird of Apollo," and, according to legend, it sang a sad and poignant song just before it died, which is where the expression "swansong" comes from. The old Greeks must've been listening to another kind of swan, though, because swan's songs sound either like a flute with laryngitis or an automobile horn with hiccups. Even the so-called "mute" swan hisses when he's angry, and calls the young with a sound like a pooped-out puppy's bark.

Swans are excellent fliers and great swimmers, which is a little difficult to imagine if all you've ever seen them do is glide majestically across a smooth pond. During the nesting season they've got dispositions like cranky crocodiles with cramps, and get pretty darned aggressive. They've been known to be extremely dangerous when teased by children or dogs, and who wouldn't be? They flail with their strong wings and batter with their big beaks, and have been known to break a full-grown man's arm by striking with the "knuckle" on the leading edge of the wing. Definitely not recommended as a pet to decorate the backyard pool, although with some kids it might not be a bad idea.

There are two kinds of swans in America, the whistling swan and the trumpeter swan, with the whistler being the smaller of the two. They range in size between fifty-two inches long and sixty-five inches long, and have wingspreads up to nine feet. They can fly as fast as sixty miles an hour and weigh over thirty-five pounds. It's not the kind of bird you'd like to have suckle its young in your cummerbund!

The nest of the swan is sometimes five feet across and made mostly of acquatic vegetation. Sometimes the nest is built on top of a vacated beaver's home. No one knows why. Maybe they like a flooded basement. In any event, Mama Swan lays between two and ten snow white eggs, then sits around for five or six weeks while papa stands guard, then watches the cygnets crack their way into the brave old world, and in no time at all she's taking them down to the water's edge for their first swimming lesson.

They're not pretty children as anyone who's ever read H. C. Anderson's charming tale of the Ugly Duckling knows. Their feathers are a dull, lackluster gray, and they waddle as though they'd ridden a horse all day. But when they get about five months old and weigh close to twenty pounds, their plumage turns a gleaming white and the regal looking swan has a proud grace and beauty all his own----just like editors after a three martini lunch.

HE'S A VERY HAPPY CAPTIVE

Tapir

Last summer someone developed a new product that was a mixture of sand, leaves, ants, flies, watermelon seeds, potato salad, and pieces of charred beef bone . . . it was called *Instant Cookout!* Old Mama Nature developed a new product too, way back when dinosaurs were puppy-sized. She whipped up an animal that looks like a streamlined pig, with feet similar to a horse's, a snout that's reminiscent of an elephant's trunk, eyes that squint like a rhinocerous's, and ears that twitch like a rabbit's. I don't know what Mama Nature called this interesting animal, but the zoologists call it a *tapir*. Nature must have been doing something right, because the tapir has survived from then till now.

Tapirs are found only in the central and northern portions of South America, and in the Malayan sectors of southern Asia, and kind of difficult to find at that because they're really active only at night. Now and then they'll stir their sturdy legs during the daylight hours and head for a nearby river, where they're more at home than most mammals. They can not only dive like a well trained aquanaut, but they can actually walk along the river floor. Why anyone would want to walk on the bottom of a river I don't know—unless you like to read the labels on beer cans.

Either the tapir is very independent or has very weak eyes because he doesn't follow any established trail, he just lowers his large head and stubbornly pushes through the forest, blazing his own trail as he bulldozes and browses. As you might guess this isn't too fast a method of movement and as a result he's easily overtaken. If he lives in Malaya, the tiger or leopard overtakes him; if he lives in Central and South America, the jaguar overtakes him. If he's near water, he has a pretty good chance of getting away, if not, he puts up a creditable fight, and then winds up as a delicacy the feline family can enjoy.

The Malayan tapir can't make up its mind what color to be and so the hind part is gray, while the legs and front part are black. The South American cousin is blackish-brownish in color and not near so sporty looking. In captivity the tapir seems quite happy, eating like a 500 pound vacuum cleaner, eating almost anything put within reach . . . vegetables, grain, meat, handkerchieves, or zoo keeper's fingers. He doesn't make much of a sound, a grunt or two now and then, and a sort of high pitched hissing cry that's reminiscent of an angry teakettle.

The baby tapir has a beauty all his own. He's born with a most intriguing pattern of stripes, and slowly loses them as he matures. The young ones look somewhat like darkly colored watermelons with legs. Besides making good eating for the natives, there's a belief that epilepsy can be cured by grinding the toenails down into a powder and swallowed. Some people will swallow anything.

HIS SIGHT IS WORSE
THAN HIS BITE

CHAS. HERZOG III

Tarantula

It all began hundreds of years ago, in southern Italy around a town called Taranto. The superstitious townsfolk almost became bowlegged from sidestepping the large, hairy spiders that seemed to skulk around the town, and occasionally someone would step on a spider instead of a grape and the startled cry "Mama mia, atsa some spicy meataball!" would ring through the town. The cry of fear was the signal for the village medicine man to start his Hippocratic magic, and since Blue Cross was unknown at the time, the next best thing to do was devise an antidote that pleased the next of kin as well as the victim.

The pseudo-medico perpetuated the myth that a person bitten by one of these hairy horrors would surely take the deep six unless he listened and danced to a special wild and exciting music. You see, the doctor was also head of the musician's union. Anyhow, the legend has died, and all that's left in southern Italy now is a lively and lovely dance called the Tarantella, and the poor spider has been a poisonous villain ever since.

The truth of the matter is that the tarantula, the insect not the dance, is much maligned, and not really deserving of his wild reputation. It's hard to believe, but there is not record of a tarantula ever killing a normal human adult. However, you can't say the same thing about some smaller animals. He's been known to knock off small birds, snakes, mice, and a now and then frog. I think it's the sight rather than the bite of this hairy eight-legged creature scuttling quietly along that causes the skin to crawl, the heart to flutter, and the knees to knock like a nervous castanet. One look and you feel as though you've just swallowed a Jello hand grenade.

The tarantulas found in the United States are very distant cousins of the Italian family, and can get up to two inches long in body length with a five inch leg spread. It's one of the world's most harmless spiders, although if you handle him roughly, he'll bite painfully, and then the danger is in infection, not venom. The United States spiders love the ground and burrow into the earth to sleep by day and hunt by night.

In South America live the largest of the species, with leg spreads of up to eight inches, and thick, rust-colored hairy bodies that sometimes measure up to four inches long. They live in trees, catch birds, and sneak into our lives via banana boats from south of the border. It's enough to make a banana split the scene!

Ah, but the love life of a tarantula! There's something to make the movie producers chortle in anticipation. A sexy horror film. The marriage of a tarantula is as dangerous as bobbing for apples in a crocodile pool----but only for the male spider! In the first place, the female is two to three times the size of the male, and in the last place, she dines on her bridgeroom as a post-nuptial meal. For that matter, if she "doesn't like his looks" she may gobble him up as he approaches her. Well sir, faced with such a predatory mate, it's a wonder there are enough foolhardy lovelorn males to go around! It's the female tarantula liberation philosophy----if you can't beat 'em, eat 'em!

Given a small aquarium (with a tight top), an occasional cricket, mouse, or worm, a drink of water now and then, and little else, a tarantula is a pretty happy house guest. Normal life spans in captivity are between ten and fifteen years, and the furry little funster will probably never give you a moment's worry. You'll probably never take him to a vet for distemper shots, never worry about mange, and—whoever heard of spaying a tarantula?

Toucan

Gregarious gourmets define "Pheasant under Glass" as a great bird with a big bill . . . ho, ho, ho! And the big bird with the big bill that piques our interest, makes an entertaining pet, eats fruit, and makes more noise than a house detective on rusty roller skates, is a Jimmy Durante-looking kind of bird called the *toucan*.

Just one look at this feathered flyer and you immediately wonder how he keeps his balance . . . after all, a nose that big makes it possible to smoke a cigar in the shower and not have it extinguished. However, big as that beak is, it weighs hardly anything at all, being made up of lightweight cells, something like corrugated cardboard, very strong but very light. The toucan really has no trouble when he's walking around, flying around, or just standing around, it's when he tries to hit the sack for a good night's sleep that he runs into a little problem. What does he do with the cumbersome beak? I guess it's sort of like joining a nudist colony for the first time . . . what do you do with your hands?

The toucan, a Latin American relative of the woodpecker, solves this minor inconvenience quite cleverly, and by the numbers. First he turns his head backward, then twists it sideways, then lays it across the top of his back, followed by spreading out his fanlike tail and folding it not only over his big peninsula of a beak, but also over his entire back! It's somewhat like describing the contortionist who played football . . . and ran around his own end!

There are thirty-seven kinds of toucans, ranging from Mexico down to Argentina, some of them with wild color patterns on their bills, some living high in the mountains of the Andes, but most of them living in the tropical forests pretty close to sea level. They gather in the high branches and chatter and clatter, berate and bugle, whistle and scream, to say nothing of tootling and trumpeting, all the while rocking back and forth as they swing their massive bills in an up and down movement for emphasis. The folks in South America say this reminds them of someone preaching to them, and so these colorful birds are sometimes called "preacher birds."

Some of the birds seem to shout "tucano-tucano" over and over, which explains in part how they got their name. They love to eat fruit or succulent seeds, but they won't turn up their beak at a juicy insect, and since they're up around other bird's nests, they'll even munch a lunch of eggs and maybe go yum-yum with a young fledgling or two.

They nest in high places in the tall trees, and fly in a slow and seemingly cumbersome manner, flapping their wings with a noisy splatter, something like a four-bladed helicopter using three blades. The largest of the family of toucans is the one called the *toco*, and he's about the size of a large crow. I'm told that these bumptious birds are easy to make pets of, all you need is a large cage, a little love, and a set of king-sized earplugs.

HERE'S A WEAK CROAKER

CHAS. HERZOG III

Tuatara

Ah, the poor tuatara, the loneliest reptile in the world, the last of his line, the last remaining representative of an almot extinct family, the only reptile that must feel as alone as a hermit with halitosis.

The tuatara, whose relatives disappeared from the face of the earth over 100 million years ago, is found only around New Zealand, nowhere else, and in a climate so cold that few other reptiles could survive because cold-blooded animals can only stand so much cold blood and then it just refuses to flow. They can't change to winter-weight blood, I guess. This little lizard-like creature used to live on the New Zealand mainland, but through the years has made his way onto jut a few tiny islands in the Bay of Plenty, and that's the last stronghold of this living fossil, the rare and retiring survivor from the times of the dinosaur.

Apparently the tuatara is a nighttime creature, like actors and weathermen, and becomes more active during the time after sunset than before. During the daylight hours he sort of lives in a burrow among the rocks, but he loves to see that evening sun go down because then it's chow time, and he slithers and slides across the bleak terrain looking for snails and crickets or other wee beasties that move slower than he does.

Not too many reptiles have voices, but the tuatara does, a kind of weak croak that sounds like a fingernail scraped over a blackboard, and sometimes at night, on a tiny islet called Stephens Island, not too far north of Auckland, they can be heard croaking a sad cacophony. It's estimated that there are still about five thousand of these disappearing animals on this one islet. Well, maybe he's not the loneliest reptile in the world at that.

There's an old story about the most bashful man in the world in that he was a fourteen month baby. But the tuartara isn't far behind. The eggs are laid in a low place in the soil, between eight and fourteen to the clutch-----but they don't hatch until twelve months later when they poke their lizardly way through the parchment-like shell and dig their way into their restricted world. They're about four and one half inches long at birth and take many, many years to grow up to their maximum length, which is about two feet long.

I don't think this remnant of when the earth was young would make a very good pet, though. First, they're hard to get; and second, they sound like they'd be hard to keep, what with the worry about the correct temperature and the right food. However, there are records at the Dublin Zoo that one hardy specimen lived for twenty-three years on a diet of earthworms and strips of raw meat. If that's a diet for survival—maybe we should all try it!

GOBBLE!

CHAS. HERZOG III

Wild Turkey

Wouldn't it be great if someone could cross a turkey with a kangaroo? Then around Thanksgiving time you could stuff the tasty critter from the outside! And wouldn't it be great if we could have wild turkeys roam our woods once again as in the days of Daniel Boone?

At one time these lordly birds were as numerous in America as ten-gallon hats in Texas, but by 1920 they were as scarce as meat in a drugstore sandwich. Our Pilgrim fathers discovered that this North American gobbler had bronze plumage, and in the bright sunlight could see his bright red wattles, coral pink legs, and iridescent feathers that glistened blue, green, and red, while the tail feathers were a rich bronze. His tame, black-legged Thanksgiving turkey cousin, is smaller, and originally came from Mexico and seems as dull as a dedication at a dental floss factory by comparison.

The nimrods of the world found the wild turkey tender and tempting, and it was just a matter of time before these feathered, two-legged banquets were both shot and trapped in great and increasing amounts. That, coupled with the lumberjack's axe and the devastating forest fires, was enough to make the gobbler population start dropping, like Dow-Jones on a bad day on Wall Street. By the turn of the century, finding a wild turkey north of the Mason-Dixon line, was like looking for a horse in horseradish. I guess Mason and Dixon had to draw the line somewhere.

Along about 1930, game conservationists in Pennsylvania decided to try and save the bird that Benjamin Franklin thought should have been our national bird, and so they live-trapped the few turkeys that were left and set them up in a cozy little light housekeeping arrangement with a few half-wild game farm hens. But old Tom was haughty and would have nothing to do with this artificial matchmaking. Not only wouldn't he breed—he wouldn't even eat! Now that's what I call independence.

The solution was relatively simple. The game wardens just built ten acre enclosures deep in the woods and brought the hens to the toms, and in just a short while the masculine ego was strutting proudly, puffing out his tufted breast, dragging his outstretched wings, shaking his passionate jowls and gobble-gobble-gobbling in no uncertain terms. Fertilized eggs by the dozens were found faster than you could say "Floccipaycinihilipilification." And so at least one bird species has been saved from "eggstinction!"

The eggs weigh about four ounces, are yellow and white with rusty speckles, and in an incubator take twenty-eight days to hatch. Over the years the half-wild birds developed into real wild turkeys, wilder than the hair in your ears, and at last count there were over 45,000 in Pennsylvania alone. They're gaining, the breed is reviving, and the hunters are rubbing their flintlocks in joy. All's well that begins well, I guess.

THEY'RE ALL TURTLES

CHAS. HERZOG III

Turtle

Ambrose Bierce, the celebrated author, once said that armor is a kind of clothing worn by a man whose tailor was a blacksmith. And the horny shell of a turtle is a kind of armor whose tailor sure knew how to design a suit that would wear well for several hundred million style changes.

Way back before there were birds or mammals, or even dinosaurs, before there were any crocodilians, lizards or snakes, there were turtles. And the strange thing about these conservative reptiles with armor, is that they look pretty much the same today as they did 200 million years ago. They still have a nice, tough dome of protection on top, called the *carapace,* and a slightly thinner plate of protection on the underside, called the *plastron,* making them look like army helmets with legs. Shelter and clothing in one compact unit, with no homeowners' policy to worry about.

There are about 300 kinds of turtles. Some live in the oceans, others live in fresh water, some divide their time between land and water, and some live on land almost exclusively. The one thing that they all have in common though, is that they all lay their eggs in holes in the earth. If the fertile turtle knew better, she wouldn't do this, because it makes the babies mighty vulnerable, both before they hatch and after they hike, falling prey to birds, dogs, rats, and other assorted predators looking for a tasty tidbit.

At first a baby turtle's shell is pretty soft, but if they survive for a while, their shells begin to harden and get thicker. The harder the shell, the better crack they have at living to a ripe old age. There are records of turtles living over a century and a half. Just think what the social security checks would look like!

What's the difference between a tortoise, turtle, and terrapin? The answer is that everybody thinks they're different, which is what makes them all alike. Actually, they're all turtles, although some folks classify tortoises as turtles that live on land, never entering water, which might make a good argument for cologne makers. Then there are the *terrapins,* a name given turtles by our own American Indians, but gourmets call them *delicious,* classifying terrapins as turtles that are finger lickin' good.

One of the tastiest, and also one of the largest of turtles is the Galápagos tortoise, a giant that can weigh in at over 500 pounds, which is even more remarkable when you consider that they eat mostly grass and sharp spined cactus, a not too nutritious kind of food. If they had teeth they could use the needles for toothpicks. Early day pirates and whalers found that these hardy, docile monsters could live for a long time without feeding, and so they packed them into the holds of their ships and had great supplies of fresh meat for their long voyages.

Regardless of what Aesop or Disney tell you, there's not a turtle in the world that could beat a hare in a footrace, even if the hare stopped off for lunch, took in a movie, or took time out to practice his multiplication tables. A man named Nichols studied the movement of these lumbering creatures that speed along slower than a snail with a snootful, and he found that a plain old box turtle roared forty-six yards in fifteen minutes. At this astounding speed he'd be galloping a full mile in a little more than nine and a half hours! Kentucky Derby material, he ain't. Of course, there are turtles that are speedier than that, but who's got the patience to time a tortoise, turtle, or terrapin, if you have to use a calendar for a stopwatch!

WAPITI THE WARRIOR

CHAS. HERZOG III

Wapiti

They say that love at first sight is that magic moment when you discover she has the same neuroses that you have . . . however, it isn't love at first, second, or even third sight that makes an American elk collect as many as fifty cows for his harem. He's just doing what comes naturally. Of course, the elk would have to be big, brawny, brave, and bombastic to collect that many cows; more likely he'd have a dozen or so females in his harem, which is still a pretty fair group to pamper and protect while savoring, soothing, and satisfying.

The only member of the deer family that's larger than the American elk is the moose, and that's going some because the elk can weigh up to 1,000 pounds and stand close to five and a half feet at the shoulder, with his antlers spreading a fearsome five feet. The Shawnee Indians gave this magnificent beast the name *Wapiti* and some folks won't give up calling the elk by the Indian name, after all, if an Indian giver gives------take!

Originally these giants of the deer family battled and browsed from southern Canada down into most of the United States, but the tremendous demand years ago for elk's teeth that could be worn on a chain to identify members of a club, caused this four-legged hatrack to be slain in wholesale numbers. Seems silly, but it's true, and that's the tooth, the whole tooth, and nothing but the tooth.

At the beginning of the mating season, when bulls are bulls and cows are darned glad of it, the male wapiti sounds his challenge, a tremendous blast called the "bugle call". The "Call" sounds something like a locomotive whistle with a bad case of laryngitis, mixed with an air raid siren, suffering from sinusitis, that reaches a shrill crescendo; after which it drops into the kind of scream you get when you step on your wife's corns; and ends with a few grunts that only another bull can interpret as a challenge. The challenger then barks a strange bark, and the battle is on.

The fight is something fierce to watch, indeed. The nostils flare, the neck swells, the eyes glaze, and both bulls charge headlong at literally "breakneck" speed. Many times the crash and impact breaks the neck of one of the aroused elk, and that seems to take all the fight out of him. However, more often than not, they'll slam at each other three or four times, and one of them will decide that the other has too many tines in his favor and, acknowledging defeat, will gallop away to fight another day. Unlike man, they know when to make a strategic withdrawal.

The enemies of the wapiti are many and varied, ranging from the puny hunter with the great gun, to wolves, coyotes, cougars, and bears, with only the little man with the big boom winning almost every encounter. A full-grown bull with a full set of antlers is usually safe from other four-legged predators. After all a 100 pound animal armed with sharp prongs on five-foot antlers is like entering a punching contest with a knife-wielding octopus. Not recommended.

The wapiti is a beautiful golden brown in color, with his head, mane, and neck a rich chestnut-brown, artistically finished off with a yellowish rump patch and a short tail bringing up the rear. In the summertime the herd never squabbles as to whether or not they'll vacation on the beach or in the mountains----they always summer in the tall timber where the mosquitoes and other insect pests leave them alone, and in the fall they head down the mountain into the valleys and meadows to live, loaf, lick, love, fight, feed, be happy, and look out for the fellow in the red jacket with the numbers on the back!

KILLER THAT'S DYING OUT

Timber Wolf

Most girls will scream at a mouse, but smile at a wolf. The two-legged variety, that is. What about the wolf that huffed and puffed and blew the house down? And what about the wolf at the door, the wolf that gobbled up Red Riding Hood's grandma, and the wolf that snuck into the sheep's clothing? An interesting animal, to say the least, and one that's certainly enriched our language. We wolf our food, and grin wolfishly. If you stay aloof you're termed a "lone wolf." If we gather in groups, we're running in a wolf pack. And don't forget who's afraid of Virginia, or maybe even the boy who cried, to say nothing of the werewolves, without which Hollywood would have had one monster less.

Almost since civilization began, man has hunted and driven the wolf, and so he's retreated as far from human habitation as he can get, surviving only in Michigan's Upper Peninsula, parts of Wisconsin, in the wilderness of Alaska, Mexico, and Canada, with a relative doing well in portions of Asia, where it's called the *Indian wolf*. Wolves, dangerous and numerous, once dotted the landscape of England in such deadly fashion in the fifteenth century that the month of January was set aside just for hunting them—and interestingly, an outlaw of that time was called a "wolf-head" . . . a criminal with a price on his head. Things haven't changed too much today, the wolf still has a price on his head and seems well on the way to extinction.

The wolf is apparently just a great big, strong, smart dog, capable of inflicting one of the most vicious bites in the animal kingdom. Although scientists continue to separate wolves into many different types, the truth of the matter is, that if you scraped all the animal off and left only the bones of a dog, a coyote, or a wolf, even the most skilled anatomist would have a hard time telling them apart.

Size is probably their most distinguishing feature, 'cause, man, they're bigger than a breadbox. Some wolves reach a weight of 175 pounds, standing 3 feet at the shoulder and getting to be 5-1/2 feet long from the tips of their naked noses to the tips of their long bush tails. The kind of animal you'd say nice doggie to, while feeling around for a club. They have relatively short ears, which in cold, cold climates help to prevent frostbite, while their king-sized tails can be curled around their cold noses and feet, protecting them from the frost when they sleep. Like setting the blanket on number 8.

To most of us a family man is one who has several small mouths to feed and one big mouth to listen to----and in the animal world strangely enough, the wolf is the model picture of the devoted mate, and family man. Usually, the male wolf, unlike the human wolf, will stay with one mate for life, unless he is forcibly separated from her. He helps the wife dig the underground den. He protects the home and family in time of danger, by first warning his brood and then drawing attention to himself to lead the enemy away or fighting to the death, and of course, he's a mighty good provider. The family ties are strong and there's a great deal of affection shown until the young are fully grown. When a member of the family is caught in a trap, the others make every effort to spring him. Admirable traits, indeed.

A wolf in the wild can reach twenty years of age, but he's sneaking up on old age when he reaches ten or twelve, and by fourteen or fifteen his teeth are usually worn down, at which point the trappers call him a "gummer." And from the stories we've heard of his ferocity, even if he doesn't have teeth, I'll bet he can still "gum" you to death.

YOU'LL NEVER FIND A MICHIGAN WOLVERINE

Wolverine

The latest status symbol is a chlorine-scented perfume----to make you smell like you own a swimming pool. However, the wolverine needs no swimming pool, and really needs no status. What he really needs is a deal with Dial soap, because, like all his relatives in the weasel family, he has scent producing glands. These glands make him smell like cooked cabbage over burnt rubber on 100 year old eggs. Ah, but the odor isn't all bad, at least not to the wolverine, because the scent helps mark the trails for him, and a short shot of wolverine "cologne" on his excess food makes is safe from other prowlers. And, paradoxically, it enchants the female wolverine. To her it smells like Arpege instead of Jockey's Paradise, and that in turn helps immeasurably in his courtship.

The wolverine is sometimes known as the *carcajou* or *skunk-bear,* but he also has another name that seems to fit him like a towel fits Brigitte Bardot. He's sometimes called the "glutton" because of his ravenous appetite. It's said that no other carnivore can eat so much in a single meal, occasionally gobbling up a whole deer in what seems to be one continuous orgy, but is really a series of closely connected meals. Wonder if he has time to brush between banquets?

The average wolverine weighs thirty or thirty-five pounds, a big one around fifty pounds, but for daring, cunning, and sheer ferocity no animal surpasses it. The wolverine is a natural born killer. When he fights, he fights to win, giving no quarter and asking no quarter, and he'd have to go to a dictionary to find the meaning of fear. They say that even the bear, the wolf, or the mountain lion will give ground when this shaggy, bearlike, three or four foot long creature moves in with sharp claws and bared teeth. And trappers aren't too thrilled with Wally Wolverine either. The traps are nothing more than a blue plate special for this voracious animal, for not only does he steal the bait and eat it, but the odds are that he'll damage the trap or carry it off somewhere as well.

The Eskimos are pretty hip to the uses for this fur, even if the furriers of the world don't use it too often. The polar people use it to trim their parkas, putting the wolverine fur around the hood and sleeves where the body moisture excapes. You see, other furs will freeze to the face and wrists when the thermometer drops so low that you have to go into the basement to read it. Wolverine fur remains the same regardless of temperature----just deodorize and wear.

There are three kinds of North American wolverines and, unfortunately they're all becoming extinct. And speaking of disappearing, no one can find any record of wolverines ever living in Michigan, although that's the nickname of the state. The soubriquet comes from the early trappers who caught the wolverine up in Canada and brought them through the port of Detroit in such amazing numbers that the nickname "Wolverine State" seemed quite apt. Good thing skunks weren't popular back then.

Zebra

There are classic riddles that have confounded and entertained man for thousands of years. Riddles that date from prebiblical times to today's times, to say nothing of the *New York Times,* and it isn't too surprising to find that some of the riddles that the Sphinx asked are still being used and still being enjoyed. For instance: What happens when you cross a bulldog with a hen? You get pooched eggs! What kind of horse can take several thousand people for a ride at the same time? A race horse! And what is black and white and red all over? A sunburned zebra!

The classic puzzle when we get to talking about zebras is: Is it a white animal with black stripes or a black animal with white stripes? Well, a great many scientists and zoologists got together and gave this question some serious thought and did some serious research, and now, once and for all, we have a final verdict. This sportsmodel horse is actually white with black stripes. See how easy it is to get smart?

It's rare when you find fish without nearby fishermen, and it's almost as rare to find zebras without nearby lions, for the zebra is the lion's first choice on the menu. And strangely enough, although the zebra can really defend himself quite well against wild dogs and other flesh eaters, once the lion knocks him down, he sort of gives up, doesn't resist very strongly, dumbly accepts his fate, and you might say, takes it "lion" down.

However, he does have several pretty good weapons like strong, fearsome teeth and hooves that are sharper than a well-honed Gillette. In addition, his eyesight is excellent and his sense of smell is better than good. But his first remarkable burst of speed when startled, is probably his best aid to survival, and then when he settles down to just running, he can clip along at close to forty miles an hour.

Oops! Almost forgot his stripes. While they're not really a weapon, they are most helpful in letting him attain the average old age of fifteen years, because in wooded areas his black and white stripes merge, melt, and blend with the branches in both sunlight and moonlight.

Zebras migrate from time to time, and when they do they fit the apt phrase "thundering herd." Hunters who've seen and heard a herd of a thousand or more of these fancily marked horses galloping wildly across the African landscape say that it's a sight not easily forgotten, actually "awe-inspiring, fascinating, and frightening."

There are three kinds of zebras running around wild today. There's Grevy's zebra, the largest of the three, getting up to between 500 and 700 pounds. Burchell's zebra, the most attractively marked of the zebras, (he looks like he's wearing psychedelic pajamas). And finally, the smallest of the striped ponies, the mountain zebra, found only in the mountains of South Africa. There was a fourth kind, the quagga, but the last of his species checked out way back in 1872, the last quagga making his way to that big corral in the sky from his stall in the London Zoo.

Zebras love to take dust baths and sand baths, rolling and rollicking on well worn rolling grounds, and seem to be short tempered. Maybe it's the sand in their shoes. Anyhow, they're hard to domesticate, mostly because they seem to tire easily. They're also sullen, stubborn, and not to be trusted, sort of like a weary weatherman whose forecast of partly sunny weather had to be shoveled off the sidewalk.

Sonny Eliot of WWJ-TV is probably best known as Detroit's weatherman extraordinaire, and as the host of "At the Zoo." He has appeared in a variety of roles on local and network radio and television programs, and in local theatres.

Charles Herzog III has produced designs and illustrations for various media. He was educated at the Cleveland School of Art, the John Huntington Polytechnic Institute, and the Society of Arts and Crafts, and has shown his work at many museums and art exhibitions in the Midwest and the South.

The manuscript was edited by Jean Spang. The book was designed by Joanne Kinney. The typeface for the text is Univers designed by Adrian Frutiger in 1957; and the display face is Optima Bold.

The text is printed on 60# Neutratext Natural paper and the book is bound in Linson 2 cloth. Manufactured in the United States of America.